Treasures of the Taylorian:

Reformation Pamphlets

Martin Luther

Ein Sendbrief vom Dolmetschen

An Open Letter on Translating

Translated by Howard Jones

Taylor Institution Library, Oxford, 2017

First published in 2017 by Taylor Institution Library

http://www.bodleian.ox.ac.uk/taylor

A number of digital downloads to accompany this edition are available from the Taylor Institution Library website. They include:

An audio recording of the *Sendbrief*
A fold-your-own pamphlet facsimile
A pdf ebook of the text
A list of suggestions for further reading

The facsimile is of: *Ein sendbrieff D. M. Lutthers. Von Dolmetzscheñ vnd Fürbit der heiligenn.* [Nuremberg: Johann Petreius for Georg Rottmaier], 1530, Taylor Institution Library, ARCH. 8°.G.1530 (9)

The cover image is from the title page of *De Biblie: vth der vthleggine Doctoris Martini Luthers yn dyth düdesche vlitich vthgesettet* [...], Lübeck: Ludwig Dietz, 1533-4, Taylor Institution Library, ARCH.2°.G.1533

Typesetting and cover design by Emma Huber, Subject Consultant for German, Taylor Institution Library

ISBN 978-0-9954564-1-9

Taylor Institution Library, St Giles, Oxford, OX1 3NA

Table of Contents

Preface: The Taylorian Pamphlets

(Emma Huber)

This series of Reformation Pamphlets is being published by the Taylor Institution Library, one of the Bodleian Libraries at the University of Oxford, to commemorate the 500th anniversary of the start of the Reformation in Europe. Each text contains a transcription of the pamphlet, a new translation into English, and a facsimile of the copy held at the Taylor Institution.

The Taylor Institution Library acquired the greater part of its significant collection of Reformation texts and pamphlets in the 19th century at the suggestion of Professor Friedrich Max Müller (1823-1900), who, although better known as an Orientalist and Professor of Comparative Philology, was also the Taylorian's second professor of Modern European Languages. The librarian, Dr Heinrich Krebs (1844-1921), a native of Darmstadt in Germany, was able to acquire many as duplicates from German libraries, notably from Heidelberg in 1878.

Further additions were made in the 1920s and 1930s and two titles were presented by Professor Hermann Georg Fiedler (1862-1945) in 1940. The library now has 436 pamphlets ranging in date between 1518 and 1589, mainly by Luther with a few by Melanchthon, Hans Sachs, Hutten and others.

We hope this series of pamphlets will bring Luther and his contemporaries to a new audience, as well as assisting students in their study of these important, revolutionary texts.

EIn Sermon oder Predig
von dem ablaſʒ vnd gnade
durch den wirdigen docto-
rem Martinum Luther Augu
stiner zu wittenbergk ge-
macht vnd gepre
diget.

The earliest Reformation pamphlet in the Taylorian collection
Ein Sermon oder Predig von dem ablaß vnd gnade, ARCH.8° G.1518 (5)

A Note on the Facsimile

(Henrike Lähnemann)

When looking at the end of the facsimile, you see a blank page. Or do you? We decided to include a scan of this textless space because it actually tells a lot about the history of the *Sendbrief*, so much so that we can talk about the 'three lives of a pamphlet'.

1. The Pocket Pamphlet

The grime on the edges and the crease in the middle of the page point to its first life: as an independent booklet, sold for not much more than a magazine today, folded by the buyer, carried in the pocket and, we imagine, passed surreptitiously between family and friends. The printing of pamphlets had increased exponentially since the controversy over Martin Luther's 95 Theses. We have included woodcut borders from one of the first pamphlets of the controversy, the German sermon on indulgences of 1518, of which there are two different copies in the Taylorian collection (cf. the image on p. v).

These pamphlets were printed on large sheets of rag paper, approximately A3-sized, with the help of a metal paper sieve. One of the lines impressed by the sieve (chainlines) is visible on the last page, running horizontally through the pencilled-in 'T'. For the printing of the *Sendbrief* there were two-and-a-half of these sheets, marked 'a', 'b', and 'c' by the printer. Each sheet would be printed with a frame into which four pages were locked so that they folded into an approximately A5-sized booklet (you can print your own version of this from the website).

The watermark, also impressed by the sieve, ended up in the gutter between the second and third page of each folded sheet (quire). It can be hard to make out, but on the last page it is a diamond shape with a cross in it, probably the top half of a more complex watermark, faintly visible as a lighter shade three quarters of the way down the right-hand edge.

To indicate to the seller or bookbinder how to fold the sheets, the sequence of pages within each of the quires (sheets) is marked. On F3 you see *a ij*, on F5 *a iij*, F9 *b*, F11 *b ij*, F13 *b iij*, F17 *c*. On each side there is also a 'catchword' which shows how the text continues on the next page.

met)muß auch durch meine feinde geföddert / vnd des Luthers
a iij buch

Example of quire mark and catchword for fol. a iij recto (= p. F5)

2. The Collectable Item

Pamphlets did not have a high survival rate: they were *zerlesen* (read to pieces), recycled, or lost. Our 'Sendbrief' survived because it was bound with other similar matter into a 'Sammelband', a composite of items which were often connected thematically. It had to pay for its survival by being cropped to fit in with the rest of the collection – the missing upper part of the top line of the last page (c ij recto = F19) bears witness to this. We do not know who did this but it was a popular practice among supporters of the Reformation to acquire a number of these booklets on similar topics and build up their own library of theological controversy. The collection must have been quite extensive since there is the shadow of what would have been a 'Ledernase' (tab made of leather) visible on the last page, making it easy to look up the single items in the composite volume.

This particular collection ended up in the University Library of Heidelberg as the stamp *Bibl: Univ: Heidelb* on the back of the first page (a j verso = F2) shows. There it was separated again when in the nineteenth century spare copies of pamphlets were sold off; hence the blue stamp with *Dvplvm* (duplicate) marking it as being for sale.

3. The Teaching Tool

The pamphlet did not enjoy its new found independence for long. In 1878 it changed hands again and moved to England. When the Taylorian acquired it, as marked in the new library stamp next to the Heidelberg one, it was bound again, and this time sewn together with a padding of sixteen leaves of wood-based modern paper and glued into a cardboard cover which then had the Taylor Institution 'ex libris' pasted on top. The numerous pencil marks give a whole history of shelfmarks between the acquisition date and the modern shelving system in which the rare or 'Arch.' material is kept in the Taylorian's own strongroom. The current numbering reflects the status of the pamphlet ('ARCH.'), the format (equivalent to a modern octavo = 8 ° volume, though historically it is a quarto format since it was folded just twice), G. for 'German', '1530' for the year of its printing, and '(9)' for the place in the sequence of German octavo pamphlets from this particular year, showing the rich crop of pamphlets among the holdings.

The empty padding pages prepared the pamphlet for teaching at the Taylorian: it became a scholarly item ready for annotations by students and scholars. Although these modern pages have been respectfully left blank, the pamphlet has been intensively studied since that time. It forms an important link between studies in Theology, Historical Linguistics, Translation Theory, and History of the Book, and regularly features in handling sessions for undergraduate and graduate students. It is thus fitting that this should be the first in a series of scholarly facsimile editions of the library's pamphlet holdings. We hope that it will encourage other colleagues to follow suit with their own editions, continuing to fulfil the pedagogical aim of the collection when it was built up in the nineteenth century.

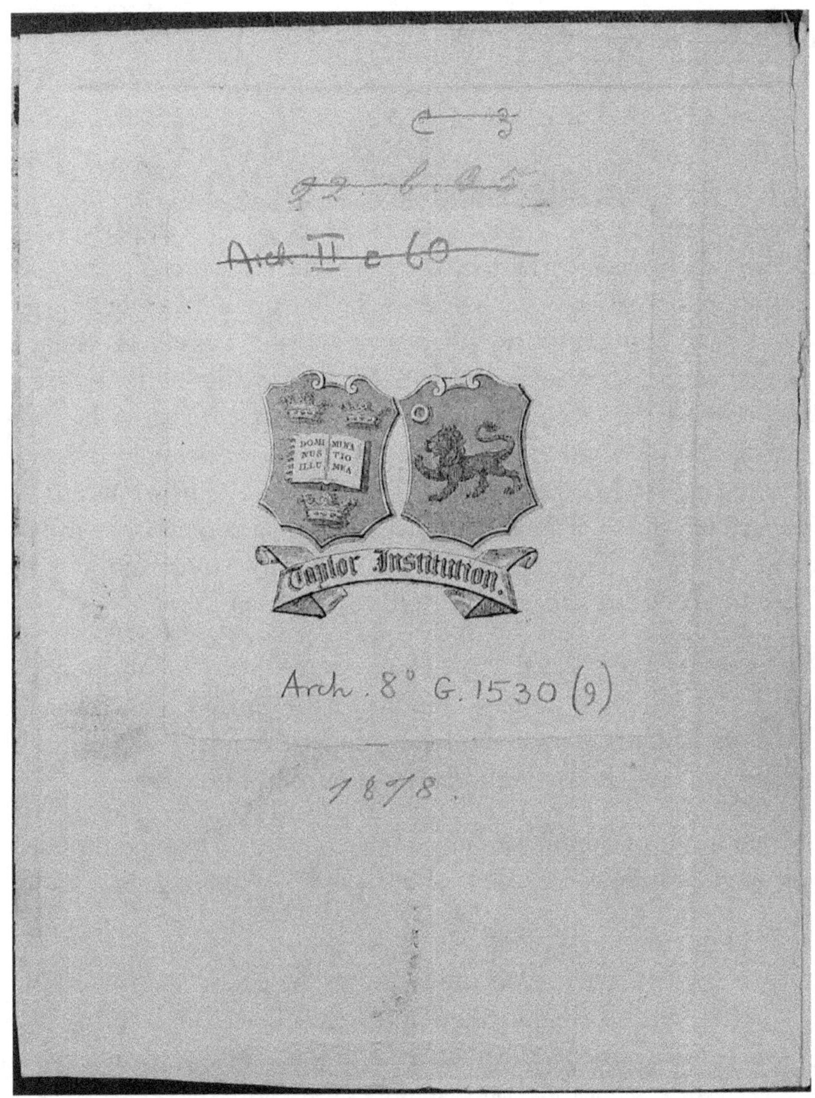

Upper pastedown of the *Sendbrief*, ARCH.8°.G.1530 (9), with the Taylor Institution crest and former shelfmarks

A Note on the Transcription

(Henrike Lähnemann)

The following is a practical guide based on my experience of teaching the *Sendbrief* and of teaching German prose translation. Early modern German was written to be performed. Luther's readers would have had exposure to German writing largely as listeners, whether through mystery plays, sermons, or public performance of the works of the 'Meistersinger'. The best approach to what may seem at first to be an impenetrable succession of prose sentences is therefore to read them aloud, particularly since Luther wrote the *Sendbrief* to argue for the importance of idiomatic expression and the 'street value' of language. You can listen to a recording of the *Sendbrief* via the website of the Taylor Institution Library.

We have not normalized the spelling, because the inconsistency is part of the reality of written German at the time. The short guide below is intended to help the modern reader decipher the transcription and enjoy the rhetorical flourish of Luther's style.

The main rule of thumb is to pronounce the words like their modern German equivalents regardless of differences in spelling.

1. Punctuation Es heiſt/Wer
   Early modern prints use full stops, brackets, question marks, and virgules as punctuation marks. The "/" *Virgel* (virgule or forward slash) is the main means of structuring sentences, and stands for both a comma and a semicolon.
   Rule of thumb: Treat a virgule like a musical caesura, to pause for breath.

2. Abbreviations Newe Teſtamēt
   Early prints took over from manuscripts some handy ways to save space. The main abbreviation mark is a dash "-". It can

be placed above any letter to replace a following *n* such as "dē" = *den* or (for Latin case endings only) an *m* such as "Christū" = *Christum*. There are also a number of established abbreviations for frequent words, mainly "dz" = *das*, "q;" = que, "vñ" = *und* and "d'" = *der*. ex fide absq; operibus
Rule of thumb: If you cannot figure out an abbreviation the first time it occurs, keep reading – they'll come up again.

3. *u/v/w – v/ſ – i/j/y*, and different *s*- and *r*-forms
   The Roman alphabet had only one symbol for *u* and *v* and one for *i* and *j*. *u/v/w* are therefore interchangeable, as are *i/j/y*, and *v/f* are both used for *f*, e.g. "vnd" = *und*; "trewe" = *treue*; "vleissig" = *fleißig*; "jhn" = *ihn*.
   Rule of thumb: pronounce *u/v/w/f/i/j/y* as in the equivalent modern German word.
   The two typographically different forms for *s* (long-*ſ* versus round-*s*) and for *r* (*r* versus *2*: bůchern nicht mehꝛ) in the print have not been distinguished in the transcription.

4. Umlaut and superscript *e* Rotzlöffel
   The umlaut sound would have been in the same position as in modern German but there is no strict rule for writing it; modern *ä* is mostly spelt as *e*, e.g. "lestern" = *lästern*; modern *ü* and *ö* are mostly spelt with a superscript *e* as in "Rotzlöffel" for *Rotzlöffel*. Sometimes umlaut is not indicated but implied, especially when *v* is used instead of *u*, e.g. "vber" for *über;* also "ſuſſe" for *süße*.
   Rule of thumb: pronounce the umlaut whenever there is one in modern German.

5. Diacritical marks above *u*
   Superscript *o* and double dots above *u* as in "bůch" for *Buch* and "saüren" for *sauren* originate from the manuscript practice of distinguishing *u* from *n* by a diacritical mark but do

not indicate a different pronunciation.
Rule of thumb: ignore diacritical marks above *u*.

6. Double versus single consonants and *s/ß, k/ck, z/tz*
There is no consistency in writing single and double consonant such as *f/ff* or *n/nn*, nor is there a difference in pronunciation, i.e. "tauffe" and "taufe" are pronounced the same. This also applies to *s* and *ß* (the latter started out as a ligature of long-*ſ* and *z* to indicate a double consonant), to *k* and *ck* (the spelling for double *k*), and to *z* and *tz*. Note that *tz* always sounds like modern German *z*, i.e. *ts*, not like English *z*.
Rule of thumb: pronounce all words like their modern German equivalents.

7. Use of *h* and *e* after vowels; long and short vowels
While in medieval German each letter would have been sounded, e.g. "lieb" would have had a diphthong in the middle, *e* after vowels had become silent in 16th century, as had *h*. In most instances a following *e* or *h* indicates a long preceding vowel, but this is not consistent, e.g. "jhm" can stand both for modern *im* and *ihm*.
Rule of thumb: pronounce all words like their modern German equivalents.

8. Word division and "Zusammenschreibung"
Hyphens in the form of "=" are used frequently but not consistently to indicate the continuation of words across line-breaks. Clear single words have been linked in the transcription but the irregular use of spaces between words such as "Esels koͤpffen" for *Eselsköpfen*, "zu rissen" for *zerrissen* or conversely "zuuerdeutschen" for *zu verdeutschen* has not been normalized.

9. Capital letters
   Capital letters are used as in English to indicate the beginning of new sentences and for proper names but also for other words such as “Sola”, “Esel” or “Testament”; these have not been normalized since they highlight key terms.

Sample transcription

Zum andern muͤgt yhr sagen/ das ich das Newe Testamēt
verdeutscht habe/ auff mein bestes vermuͤgen vnd auff mein ge
wissen/habe damit niemand gezwungen / das ers lese / sondern
frey gelasen/vnd allein zu dienst gethan denen/die es nicht besser
machen koͤnnen/ Ist niemandt verboten ein bessers zu machen.

Sendbrief, top of p. F4 in this edition

> Zum andern muͤgt yhr sagen / das ich das Newe Testamēt
> verdeutscht habe / auff mein bestes vermuͤgen vnd auff mein ge
> wissen / habe damit niemand gezwungen / das ers lese / sondern
> frey gelasen / vnd allein zu dienst gethan denen / die es nicht besser
> machen koͤnnen / Ist niemandt verboten ein bessers zu machen.

The equivalent modern German text with normalized punctuation, capitalisation, no abbreviations, and umlaut:

> Zum andern mögt ihr sagen, dass ich das Neue Testament verdeutscht habe auf mein bestes Vermögen und auf mein Gewissen; habe damit niemand gezwungen, dass er’s lese, sondern frei gelassen und allein zu Dienst getan denen, die es nicht besser machen können; ist niemand verboten, ein bessers zu machen.

Background to the Work

(Howard Jones)

1. The significance of the *Sendbrief*[1]

Martin Luther's German translation unlocked the Bible for the millions of his contemporaries who did not understand Latin. It was not the first German version of the Bible, or even the first in print, but it was the first to reach a mass audience. Given Luther's belief in 'sola scriptura', that is, scripture as the sole medium for the word of God, the translation of the Bible was an enactment of his own theology. A vernacular Bible in the hands of the laity was also a powerful weapon to challenge Church practices which had no scriptural basis.

It was not just the fact that Luther translated the Bible that was important: it was also the way he did it. Like others before him, Luther cultivated a sense-for-sense, as opposed to a word-for-word, approach. His great innovation was a translation style close in register to colloquial speech, but with a simple eloquence that brought the original text alive. The language of Luther's Bible was so influential that even his opponents, Catholic and Protestant alike, used it as the basis for their own rival versions. Luther's German Bible was to serve for centuries as a model of grammar and style, and to play a foundational part in the development of the standard language.

In the *Sendbrief* Luther offers general advice on translation as well as a defence of some of the specific translation choices he made in his German New Testament. From these it becomes clear what his guiding principles were as a translator: an intimate knowledge of the

---

[1] The full name in modern German is *Ein Sendbrief vom Dolmetschen und Fürbitte der Heiligen* (*An Open Letter on Translating and the Intercession of Saints*). For brevity we refer to the work as the *Sendbrief*.

source and target language, a feel for the idiom of both, and an understanding of the author's purpose. The same questions preoccupy translators today, whether they are working with sacred texts or not. The *Sendbrief* affords us a glimpse into the translation technique of one its most successful exponents.

The *Sendbrief* also gives us a taste of Luther's style and method of argument. His syntax and vocabulary are plain and direct, his tone sometimes academic but more often informal, and the text is interspersed with colourful turns of phrase. His arguments are, in keeping with academic discourse at the time, a combination of appeals to reason or authority, ridicule, and invective. In the *Sendbrief* we have Luther, at one point, analysing the Hebrew, Greek, and Latin precedents to argue against the translation, 'Mary, full of grace', and, at another, summarizing his attitude to Dr Snotty-Nose and his other detractors as follows: 'The fact is, a donkey doesn't need to do much braying: you just have to look at his ears'.

2. The immediate circumstances of the *Sendbrief*

Luther wrote the *Sendbrief* in September 1530 at the fortress of Coburg in Saxony. At this time the Imperial Diet (i.e. assembly) was taking place some 200 km away at Augsburg, where Luther's colleague Melanchthon was making a formal proclamation of Protestantism, the Augsburg Confession. Luther did not attend, as he had been declared an outlaw at the Diet of Worms in 1521, and was relatively safe only in Saxony under the protection first, of the supportive Frederick the Wise, Elector of Saxony (d. 1525), and then of Frederick's brother Johann, Elector since 1525. As well as corresponding with Melanchthon and his other colleagues at Augsburg, Luther spent his confinement at Coburg working on his translation of the Old Testament and on polemical writings such as the *Sendbrief*.

The pretext for the *Sendbrief* is that an anonymous (and possibly fictitious) friend of Luther's has asked for guidance on two matters: (i) why Luther inserted the word 'alone' ('allein') in his translation of

Romans 3: 28, so that it reads, 'man is justified without the works of the law, by faith alone' and (ii) whether the saints intercede by prayer in human affairs. Luther focuses mainly on the first of these topics, and uses the *Sendbrief* to set out his views on translation.

On 12 September 1530 Luther sent the manuscript to his friend Wenceslaus Linck of Nuremberg with instructions for its publication. Linck had the text printed there with a foreword of his own dated 15 September 1530.

The text reproduced here is the earliest surviving print, the so-called 'A' text, the printer of which is not named.[2] The next print, the 'B' text, was printed by Georg Rhaw at Wittenberg (where Luther was Professor of Theology), also in 1530. The B print appears to be based closely on A, but there are differences which make it possible that B was in fact copied from a (now lost) predecessor of A.

3. The controversy over Luther's Bible translation

Luther's translation of the New Testament was a bestseller when it first appeared in September 1522: the initial run of 3,000–5,000 copies sold out within weeks at a price equivalent to a labourer's weekly wage, and a revised edition was published in December. By 1525, 14 authorized and 66 unauthorized versions had appeared. At the same time as he was writing the *Sendbrief*, Luther was completing the translation of the Old Testament, parts of which had already been published in instalments. Luther's first complete Bible translation was to appear in 1534.

Why was this controversial? During the Middle Ages there were few vernacular translations of the whole Bible. This suited the Catholic Church, which considered vernacular languages inferior to the sacred languages of Latin, Greek, and Hebrew, and which, by

---

[2] Full information on the print is available in the *Verzeichnis der im deutschen Sprachbereich erschienenen Drucke des 16. Jahrhunderts* (VD 16), online as vd16.de under VD16 L 5950.

keeping the Bible in Latin, could maintain a monopoly on interpretation. Even after the appearance of printed German Bibles in the late fifteenth century, there is no evidence of widespread demand for Holy Scripture in this form, and the Bible continued to be accessible largely through verse adaptations, sermons, and selected readings. This all changed with Luther's translation: now massive public attention was focused on the Bible in a version which the Church found unsuitably informal in tone and heretical in content. The Church's objections were written up in 1523 in a critique by Hieronymus Emser (see Glossary of Names), who produced a corrected version of Luther's New Testament in 1527. We discuss in Section 4 below the particular translation choices which Luther defends in the *Sendbrief*. First we summarize the theological reasons why they were controversial.

The terms relevant to this controversy are faith, grace, justification, and works. Luther and his opponents agreed that people are justified (or, as he sometimes puts it in the *Sendbrief*, 'become righteous') by God's grace, but they disagreed about how.[3] The official Church position was that a person is justified by a combination of faith in Christ and works, i.e. deeds. Luther, by contrast, held that a person is justified by faith alone. Moreover, while his opponents believed that, when people are justified, divine grace is infused into them, altering them intrinsically, Luther held that grace is a favour which is imputed to people but remains outside them. Luther's belief that works do not help people to justification applied both to good works (good deeds done in accordance with Christian teaching) and to the works of the law (acts such as circumcision performed in fulfilment of Old Testament law). In Luther's theology, people who are justified are by nature inclined to carry out good works, so justification is the cause, rather than the effect, of such works.

A further point of contention between Luther and his opponents

---

[3] Justification/righteousness is necessary for salvation, that is, the saving of the soul from sin and death.

which is relevant to the *Sendbrief* is the authority of Scripture. For Luther's opponents, Scripture meant the Vulgate, the Latin Bible translated from Hebrew and Greek by St Jerome in the fourth century. When Erasmus published his Greek–Latin parallel edition of the New Testament in 1516 (with a second edition in 1519), the Church did not object to this as a scholarly exercise, as long as it did not undermine the authority of the Vulgate or the Church's own interpretation of it. For Luther, by contrast, Scripture meant the Bible in its original languages rather than the Vulgate, and Scripture was the sole authority. Luther made great use of Erasmus's text of the New Testament in preparing his German version, and in many cases bypassed the Vulgate where he believed it to be based on a faulty reading of the Greek.

Away from the scholarly debates about ancient Biblical languages, Luther appealed to the authority of Scripture in a more obvious way, by condemning Church practices which had no scriptural basis at all. This he did most famously by attacking indulgences in his *Ninety-Five Theses* of 1517. Originally granted by the Church in recognition of the good deeds for which people's punishments after death would be reduced, by Luther's time indulgences were being widely sold to finance the Church itself, and in particular the building of St Peter's at Rome. The latter part of the *Sendbrief* (from p. 37)[4] is devoted to another practice encouraged by the Church which Luther considered to be without scriptural authority, namely asking departed saints to intercede on behalf of the living.

However, the most controversial aspect of Luther's position on Scripture was his belief in 'sola scriptura', for this turned his translation of the Bible into a challenge to the legitimacy of the Church itself.

4. Luther's discussion of translation in the *Sendbrief*

In the *Sendbrief* Luther offers general advice on Bible translation, and

[4] Page numbers refer to the translation.

comments on specific examples. His general advice can be summarized under the following headings:

The qualities of a good translation. Luther stresses the need for an accessible, idiomatic version which reflects spoken German rather than being a word-for-word rendering of the Latin text; see especially p. 17.

The qualities of a good translator. A translator must have a deep understanding of both the source and the target language and must be a true Christian (that is, one who shares Luther's own theological viewpoint); see especially pp. 27–9.

The best method of translating. Here Luther recommends: close observation of how ordinary Germans speak; patience and hard work; and collaboration with expert colleagues; see especially pp. 15–17.

The German rendering which receives the most attention in the *Sendbrief* is (p. 5):

> Latin: *Arbitramur hominem iustificari ex fide absque operibus*[5] (Romans 3: 28)
>
> ('We consider man to be justified by faith and without works')
>
> Luther: *Wir halten / das der mensch gerecht werde on des gesetzs werck / allein durch den glauben*
>
> ('We consider that man is justified without the works of the

---

[5] The Latin which Luther cites here is not the wording of the Vulgate. It is close to that of Erasmus's 1516 and 1519 editions of the New Testament, but it is not an exact quotation from Erasmus (for example, it does not include the Latin for 'of the law'). Luther appears to be giving an approximate quotation from memory, but the omission may reflect the close association in Luther's mind between 'works of the law' and 'works' in general.

law, by faith alone')

The contentious point here is the addition of 'allein' ('alone/only'), which Luther insists upon even though there is no equivalent in either the Latin version or the Greek original.[6] Luther starts by defending this addition on grounds of idiom: in German it is more natural when *x* is affirmed and *y* denied to say 'only *x* and not *y*' rather than '*x* and not *y*' (p. 17). What Luther does not say here is that, if there is an (unstated) alternative beyond *x* and *y*, such as *z*, then specifying 'only *x*' also changes the meaning by ruling out not just *y*, but *z* too. Thus, if faith (*x*) and the works of the law (*y*) are the only alternatives, specifying 'faith alone' rather than merely 'faith' does not change the meaning. But Luther's opponents, including Emser, believed that there was an alternative to faith and the works of the law, namely good works (*z*), and that good works (along with faith) *are* necessary for justification (see Section 2 above).[7] For Luther's opponents, therefore, the addition of 'alone' is not – or not only – a question of idiom, but changes the meaning. Later in the *Sendbrief* Luther does make the theological case for adding 'only'. In contrast to Emser's distinction between the works of the law and good works, Luther presents the works of the law as the epitome of all works (see p. 29), so that when St Paul excludes the works of the law as a means to justification, all works, including good works, are excluded by implication.[8]

The other German rendering discussed in the *Sendbrief* which appears to have a theological motivation is (p. 21):

---

[6] Note that Luther also stresses the exclusiveness of faith by moving 'by faith alone' to the end of the sentence.

[7] Emser makes this distinction in a gloss to this passage of Romans in his 1527 version of the New Testament.

[8] The importance that Luther attaches to the addition of 'only' in Romans 3: 28 is inconsistent with his translation of Galatians 2: 16, where he renders a very similar Latin sentence without adding 'alone'.

Latin: *Ave, gratia plena* (Luke 1: 28)
('Hail, woman full of grace')

Luther: *Gegrusset seystu, holdselige* (September 1522)
('Greetings, gracious one')

Luther objects to a word-for-word translation from the Latin here on grounds of idiom, arguing that 'full of grace' would not be readily understood and would conjure up images such as 'a barrel full of beer or a bag full of money'. However, elsewhere Luther does use 'full' with abstract nouns, and in John 1: 14 he even calls Jesus 'full of grace', which reduces the weight of his linguistic argument. Indeed, although Luther does not say so, it is likely that his avoidance of 'full of grace' was theologically motivated. As explained in Section 3 above, Luther held that grace did not exist in people, but remained outside them. Moreover, Emser had attacked Luther's translation of this verse in his 1523 critique, arguing that, although 'gratia' could mean worldly 'favour', it had a divine sense when referring to God's grace, as here.[9]

The original Greek word underlying the Latin 'gratia plena' is 'kecharitōmenē', 'beloved, endowed with favour/grace'. Luther (p. 23) takes this word to be St Luke's attempt to render a Hebrew word meaning 'beloved, valued' which occurs in 'Ish Chamudot' 'man greatly loved/valued' in the Old Testament Book of Daniel (e.g. Daniel 9: 23). In the Vulgate version of Daniel this greeting is rendered as 'vir desideriorum'. Luther mockingly points out that a word-for-word translation of this phrase into German would be 'man of desires' ('man der lüste'), which would misleadingly suggest that Daniel was a sinful pleasure-seeker. It is noticeable that Luther's

[9] Luther is being especially provocative here, in that his translation implies a denial that divine grace exists even in the Virgin Mary. Although a saint, she was a human being and therefore, to Luther, lacked the divine quality which would be implied if she were held to be 'full of grace'.

case against the word-for-word translation 'Mary, full of grace' includes an appeal to clear, idiomatic German as well as a detailed analysis of the underlying Greek and Hebrew, but that the theological argument that grace cannot exist in people is not actually stated.

Luther rejects a word-for-word translation of the Latin in three further cases. Thus 'abundance of heart' (Matthew 12: 34, Luke 6: 45) strikes Luther as unidiomatic (p. 19), while 'loss of ointment' (Matthew 26: 8, Mark 14: 4) erroneously suggests that the ointment poured over Jesus' head has been mislaid (p. 19). In the translation discussed on p. 27 Luther also recommends a departure from the Latin, but this time at the expense of idiomatic German. Here he defends his use of a verb meaning 'to seal' rather than one meaning 'to indicate' in, 'This is the man whom God the Father has sealed' (John 6: 27). In doing so, Luther keeps closer to the sense of the Greek 'esphragisen' 'sealed', than to that of the Latin 'signavit', which can mean 'sealed' but also has a wider meaning of 'indicated'. Luther believed that 'sealed' had the special sense of 'endowed with the Holy Spirit', which he wants to preserve even though he considers that a translation closer to the Latin would have sounded better in German.

Although Luther had a clear interest in language for its own sake, all of his pronouncements on translation in the *Sendbrief* can be viewed in terms of his own theology. Luther's views on justification and grace are clear in his choice of wording in Romans 3: 28 and Luke 1: 28. His belief in the authority of the original scriptural languages is reflected in the discussion of Luke 1: 28 (together with the angel Gabriel's greeting in the Book of Daniel) and in his choice of 'to seal' in John 6: 27. More generally, Luther's belief in 'sola scriptura' underlies his general preference for accessible German: if the Bible is to serve as the unique medium with God, it must be written in an idiom which the people can understand.

5. A note on the translation provided here

The translation of the *Sendbrief* is intended to be close enough to help readers follow the German on the facing page, while conveying in English something of Luther's style (see Section 1 above).[10] Proverbs and sayings have been translated closely where they seem to work in English, but otherwise an equivalent with a similar underlying meaning has been given and a more literal translation provided in a footnote.

6. Suggestions for further reading

There is a vast literature on Luther's theory and practice of translation as well as on the legacy of his German Bible. For up-to-date suggestions for further reading, go to www.bodleian.ox.ac.uk/taylor and enter 'Sendbrief bibliography' in the 'Search' box.

7. Acknowledgements

Henrike Lähnemann and Emma Huber each wrote some of the introductory material, but I should also like to thank them for their enormous help with the rest. Henrike made countless improvements to the translation and Emma very skilfully brought the very different parts together into a coherent whole. I am also grateful for the excellent suggestions of Jeffrey Ashcroft, John Flood, Anna Linton, Alastair Matthews, Charlotte Methuen, Edmund Wareham, Helen Warner, and Chris Wells.

[10] Luther's simple and direct style can be seen by contrasting it with the more formal preface by Wenceslas Linck.

Martin Luther

Ein Sendbrief vom Dolmetschen

An Open Letter on Translating

Transcription and Translation

Ein sendbrieff D. M. Lutthers. Von Dolmetzschen vnd Fuͤrbit der heiligenn. M.D.XXX.
Wenczeslaus Linck allen Christglaubigenn

GOttes gnad vnd barmhertzigkeit. Der weise Salomon spricht Prou. 11: Wer korn inhelt / dem fluchen die leute. Aber segē kompt vber den / so es verkaufft. Welcher spruch eigentlich zu vorstehen ist von allem das zu gemeinem nutze odder troͤste der Christenheit dienen kan. Darumb schilt auch der Herr jm Euangelio den vntrewen knecht einen faulen schalck / das er sein gelt in die erden vergraben vnd verborgen hatte.[11] Solchen fluch des herren vnd der gantzen gemein zu vermeiden / hab jch diesen sendtbrieff / der mir durch einen guten freundt zu handen kommen / nit wissen zu verhalten / sonder offentlich in druck geben / Dann die weil der verdolmetzschunge halben / altes vnnd newes testaments / vil rede sich zutragen / Nemlich die feinde der warheit furgeben / sam were der text an vilen orten geendert / odder auch verfelschet / da durch viel einfeltige Christen / auch vntern gelerten / ßo der Hebreischen vnnd Grekischen sprache nit kundig / entsatzunge odder schew gewinnen / Ist guͤttlich zu verhoffen das auffs minste zum teil hie mit den gottlosen / jhr lestern vorhindert / vnnd den frommen jhr scrupel benommen sollen werden / Villeicht auch verursachet / das ettwas mehrers auff solche frag stuck odder materi / geschriben werde / Bitt der halben einen ieden liebhaber der warheit / woͤlle jhm sollich werck jm besten lassen entpfolhen sein / vnd Gott treulich bitten vmb rechten vorstandt der Goͤttlichen schrifft zu besserung vnnd meherung gmeiner Christenheit. Amen. Zu Nuͤrmberg am 15. Septembris. Anno 1530.

[11] Matthew 25: 14-30 (the Parable of the Talents).

An open letter by Dr Martin Luther on translating and the intercession of saints 1530

Wenceslas Linck to all believers in Christ[12]

I wish you God's grace and mercy. The wise Solomon says (Proverbs 11: 26), 'People curse the man who holds back grain, but bless the man who sells it.' These words should properly be understood to apply to anything that can contribute to the general benefit and well-being of Christians. This is also the reason why, in the Gospel, the Lord rebukes the faithless servant and calls him an idle wretch for hiding his money in the ground. To avoid being similarly cursed by the Lord as well as by all Christians I have decided not to withhold this open letter, which came into my hands through a good friend, but to go into print with it. Since there has been a lot of discussion about translating the Old and New Testaments, and particularly as the enemies of the truth are making out that the text of the Bible has been altered or even falsified in several places, causing many ordinary Christians, even educated ones who do not know Hebrew or Greek, to be horrified and shy away, it is sincerely to be hoped that this publication will go at least some way to putting an end to the slanders of the godless and dispelling the concerns of the devout. Perhaps it will also lead to further writing on points of contention and subjects like this. I therefore beg all lovers of the truth to give this work an enthusiastic welcome and to ask God faithfully for a right understanding of divine Scripture – for the improvement and increase of the whole of Christianity. Amen.

Nuremberg. September 15, 1530

---

[12] A friend and ally of Luther's. For this and other names in the text, including nicknames, see Glossary of Names.

Dem Erbarn vnd fursichtigen N. meinem guͤnstigen Herrn vnd freunde.

GNad vnd fride in Christo / Erber fursichtiger lieber Herr vñ freund / ich hab ewer schrifft entpfangen mit den zwo questionen odder fragen / darin yhr meines berichts begert. Erstlich warumb ich zun Roͤmern am dritten capitel / die wort S. Pauli Arbitramur hominem iustificari ex fide absq; operibus /[13] also verdeutsch habe. Wir halten / das der mensch gerecht werde on des gesetzs werck / allein durch den glauben / Vñ zeigt danebẽ an / wie die Papisten sich vber die massen vnnuͤtze machen / weil ym text Pauli nicht stehet das wort Sola (Allein) vnd sey solcher zusatz von mir nicht zu leiden ynn Gottes wortten &c. Zum andern / ob auch die verstorben Heiligen fur vns bitten / weil wir lesen / das ja die Engel fur vns bitten &c. Auff die ersten frage (wo es euch gelustet) muͤgt yr ewern Papisten von meinet wegẽ antworten also.

Zum ersten / Wenn ich D. Luther mich hette muͤgen des versehen / das die Papisten alle auff einen hauffen so geschickt werẽ / dz sie ein Capitel yn der schrifft kuͤndten recht vnd wol verteutschen / So wolt ich furwar mich der demut haben finden lassen / vñ sie vmb hilff vnd beystand gebeten das Newe Testament zuuerteutschen. Aber die weil ich gewuͤst / vnd noch vor augen sihe / das yhr keiner recht weiß / wie man dolmetschen / odder teutsch reden sol / hab ich sie vnd mich solcher muͤhe vberhaben / Das merckt man aber wol / das sie aus meinem dolmetschen vnd teutsch / lernen teutsch reden vñ schreiben / vñ stelen mir also meine sprache / dauon sie zuuor wenig gewist / dancken mir aber nicht dafur / sondern brauchen sie viel lieber wider mich.

---

[13] 'We consider man to be justified by faith and without works' (Romans 3: 28).

To the honourable and wise 'N', my generous patron and friend.[14]

I wish you grace and peace in Christ, my honourable, wise, dear patron and friend! I have received your letter asking me for guidance on those two *quaestiones*, i.e. discussion-points. First, why I rendered the words of St Paul in Romans Chapter 3: 28, 'Arbitramur hominem iustificari ex fide absque operibus', into German as 'We consider that man is justified without the works of the law, by faith alone'[15] – and you also point out what a huge fuss the papists are making because the word 'sola' ('alone') is not in Paul's text, and my addition here to the words of God cannot be tolerated, etc. Secondly, whether the departed saints pray for us, since we *do* read that the angels pray for us, etc. On the first question you can, if you like, pass onto your papists the following answer from me.

First of all: If I, Dr Martin Luther, could have imagined that all the papists between them possessed enough talent to put a single chapter of Scripture into decent, proper German, I would certainly have had the humility to ask for their help and support with my German version of the New Testament. However, knowing as I did – and the evidence is still before my eyes – that not one of them has a clue how to translate or how to speak German, I spared them and myself the bother. But it's quite obvious that they're using my translation, my German, to learn how to speak and write German themselves, and in doing so stealing a language which belongs to me and which they knew little about before. Yet rather than thanking me for it they prefer to use it against me.

---

[14] 'N' stands for 'Non Nominatus', Latin for 'not named'.

[15] For the meaning of 'justified', 'works of the law', and 'faith' in Luther's theology, as well as a discussion of Luther's translation here, see Background, Sections 3 and 4.

Aber ich gan es jn wol / den es thut mir doch sanfft / dz ich auch meine undāckbare jůnger dazu meine feinde reden gelert habe.

Zum andern můgt yhr sagen / das ich das Newe Testamēt verdeutscht habe / auff mein bestes vermůgen vnd auff mein gewissen / habe damit niemand gezwungen / das ers lese / sondern frey gelasen / vnd allein zu dienst gethan denen / die es nicht besser machen kůnnen / Ist niemandt verboten ein bessers zu machen. Wers nicht lesen wil / der las es ligen / ich bite vnd feyre niemādt drumb. Es ist mein testament vnd mein dolmetschung / vnd sol mein bleiben vnnd sein. Hab ich drinnen etwa gefeilet (das mir doch nicht bewůst / vnd freilich vngern einen bůchstaben mütwilliglich wolt vnrecht verdolmetschen) darůber wil ich die Papistē nicht zu richter leiden/ denn sie haben noch zur zeit zu lange ohren dazu / vnd yhr ycka ycka ist zu schwach mein verdolmetschen zu vrteilen / Ich weiß wol / vnd sie wissens weniger / denn des Mülners thier / was fur kunst / fleiß / vernunfft / verstandt zum gutten dolmetscher gehůret / denn sie habens nicht versůcht.

Es heist / Wer am wege bawet / der hat viel meister. Also gehet mirs auch. Die jhenigen die noch nye haben recht reden kůnnen / schweige deñ dolmetschen / die sind allzumal meine meister / vnd ich mus yhr aller junger sein. Vnd wenn ich sie hette sollen fragen / wie man die ersten zwey wort Matthei 1. Liber Generationis[16] solte verdeutschen / so hette yhr keiner gewist gack dazu zu sagen / Vnd vrteilen mir nu das gantze werck / die feinen gesellē.

[16] 'The Book of the Genealogy (of Christ)'; these are the opening words of the New Testament (Matthew 1:1).

Still, I don't begrudge them this at all, because I have to say it tickles me that I've actually taught my own ungrateful disciples, indeed my enemies, how to speak.

Secondly, you can tell them that I've rendered the New Testament into German conscientiously and as well as I could, and I haven't forced anyone to read it, but given them the choice, and done it purely as a service to those unable to do better themselves. There's nothing to stop anyone from improving on it. People should leave it alone if they don't want to read it: I'm not asking anyone to, nor praising anyone who does. This text and this translation are mine and mine alone, now and forever. Even if there are places where I've made mistakes – not that I'm aware of any, and of course I would be loath wilfully to mistranslate a single letter – I won't have the papists sitting in judgement on it: their ears are still too long, and their hee-hawing too feeble for them to pronounce on my translation.[17] I have a very good idea of the sort of skill, hard work, sense, and intelligence it takes to be a good translator, and they have less idea than a beast of burden,[18] since they've never tried it.

As the saying goes, 'A builder's work is judged by every passer-by',[19] and that's what's happening to me. The very same people who have never been able to speak properly, let alone translate, are suddenly my masters, and I've got to be a disciple to them all. And if I'd asked them how to put into German the first two words of Matthew 1, *Liber Generationis*, not one of them would have managed so much as a 'Quack', and now they're passing judgement on my entire work, the excellent fellows.

---

[17] This is the first of the many comparisons which Luther makes between his detractors and donkeys, proverbially stupid animals, then as now.

[18] Literally: 'a miller's animal'.

[19] Literally: 'He who builds by the roadside has many masters.'

Also gieḡ es S. Hieronymo auch / da er die Biblia dolmetscht / da war alle welt sein meister / Er allein war es / der nichts kunte / Vnd vrteileten dem guten man sein werck / die jhenigē / so ym nicht gnug gewest weren / das sie ym die schuch hetten sollē wischen / Darumb gehőret grosse gedult dazu / so yemād etwas offentlich guts thun will / denn die wellt wil meister klűglin bleiben / vnd mus ymer das Ros vnter dem schwantz zeumen / alles meistern / vnnd selbs nichts kőnnen / das ist yhr art / dauon sie nicht lassen kan.

Ich wolt noch gern den Papisten ansehē / der sich erfur thet / vnd etwa eine epistel S. Pauli oder einen Propheten verdeutschet / So fern / das er des Lűthers teutsch vñ dolmetzschen nicht dazu gebraucht / da solt man sehen ein fein / schőn / loblich deutsch odder dolmetzschen / Deñ wir haben ja gesehē den Sudler zu Dresen / der mein New Testament gemeistert hat (ich wil seinen namen yn meinen bűchern nicht mehr nennen / So hat er auch nun seinen richter / vnd ist sonst wol bekandt) der bekennet / das mein deutsch susse vnd gut sey / vnd sahe wol / das ers nicht besser machen kundt / vñ wolt es doch zu schandē machen / fur zu / vnd nam fur sich mein New Testament / fast von wort zu wort / wie ichs gemacht hab / vnd thet meine vorrhede / gloß vnd namen dauon / schreib seinen namen / vorrhede vnd gloß dazu / verkaufft also mein New Testament vnter seinem namen / Wañ / liebē kinder / wie geschach mir da so wehe / da sein landsfurst mit einer grewlichen vorrhede verdampt / vnd verbot des Luthers New Testament zu lesen / Doch daneben gebot des Sudelers New Testament zu lesen / welchs doch eben dasselbig ist / das der Luther gemacht hat.

The same happened to St Jerome when he translated the Bible: everybody else was his master, and he was the only one who didn't know what he was doing, yet those passing judgement on the good man's work weren't worthy to wipe his shoes. So it takes a lot of patience to do any public good – everyone's always trying to be such a know-it-all, and then they invariably put the cart before the horse themselves,[20] acting as the masters in everything, yet capable of nothing themselves – that's just the way people are: they can't help it.

I'd just like to see a papist come out and produce a German version of any one of St Paul's epistles or the Prophets![21] If he weren't using Luther's German translation, we'd be sure to get a translation into fine, charming, delightful German. As you know, there was the Bungler of Dresden, who criticized my New Testament (and I'm not going to mention his name again in writing, as he's met his final Judge by now and is in any case well known)[22] – he acknowledged the pleasing quality of my German, and clearly saw that he wouldn't be able to improve on it himself, and yet he was still keen to discredit it, so off he went and helped himself to my New Testament almost word for word as I had written it, took out my preface, commentary, and name, put in his preface, commentary, and name, and that way sold my New Testament as his own work. Oh, dear children, it was so distressing when the Bungler's prince,[23] in a most unpleasant preface, condemned Luther's New Testament and banned people from reading it, while at the same time ordering them to read the Bungler's New Testament, which is exactly the same as the one produced by Luther!

---

[20] Literally: 'bridle the horse under its tail (as opposed to its head)'.

[21] At the time of writing the *Sendbrief*, Luther was working on the translation of the Old Testament Prophets.

[22] Hieronymus Emser; see Glossary of Names.

[23] Duke George of Saxony; see Glossary of Names.

Vnd das nicht yemand hie dencke / ich liege / So nym beide Testament fur dich / des Luthers vnd des Sudelers / halt sie gegen ein ander / so wirstu sehē / wer yn allen beidē der dolmetzscher sey / Denn was er yn wenig orten geflickt vnd geendert hat (wie wol mirs nicht alles gefellet) So kan ichs doch wol leiden / vnnd schadet mir sonderlich nichts / so viel es den text betrifft / darumb ich auch nie da wider hab woͤllen schreiben / sondern hab der grossen weißheit muͤssen lachen / das man mein New Testament so grewlich gelestert / verdampt / verboten hat / weil es vnter meinē namen ist außgangen / Aber doch muͤssen lesen / weil es vnter eines andern namen ist außgangen. Wie wol / was das fur ein tugent sey / einem andern sein bůch lestern vnd schenden / darnach das selbige stelen / vnd vnter eigenem namen dennoch auß lassen gehen / vnd also durch frembde verlesterte erbeyt eygen lob vnd namen suͤchen / das las ich seinen richter finden. Mir ist ynn des gnug / vnd bin fro / das meine erbeit (wie S. Paulus auch rhuͤmet) [24] muß auch durch meine feinde gefoͤddert / vnd des Luthers bůch on Luthers namen / vnter seiner feinde namen gelesen werden / Wie kuͤnd ich mich bas rechen?

Vnd das ich wider zur sachen kome / Wañ ewr Papist sich vil vnnuͤtze machen wil mit dem wort (Sola Allein) so sagt jm flugs also / Doctor Martinus Luther wils also haben / vnnd spricht / Papist vnd Esel sey ein ding. Sic volo / sic iubeo / sit pro ratione voluntas. Denn wir woͤllen nicht der Papisten schuler noch juͤnger / sonder yhre meister vnd richter sein / Woͤllen auch ein mal stoltziern vñ pochen mit den Esels koͤpffen / vñ wie Paulus wider seine tollen Heiligen sich rhuͤmet[25] / so wil ich mich auch widder diese meine Esel rhuͤmen. Sie sind doctores? Ich auch. Sie sind gelert? Ich auch. Sie sind Prediger? Ich auch. Sie sind Theologi? Ich auch. Sie sind Disputatores? Ich auch. Sie sind Philosopi? Ich auch. Sie sind Dialectici?

---

[24] Philippians 1: 18.

[25] 2 Corinthians 11: 21-3.

And just so no-one thinks I'm lying, take the two versions for yourself, Luther's and the Bungler's, compare them, and you'll see who is the translator in both cases. There are a few places where he's made changes and stitched together parts of my version, and even though I don't like everything he's done, I can still live with it and it doesn't particularly bother me as far as the text is concerned, which is why I was never planning to put my objections in writing, though I had to laugh at the excellent judgement of so seriously slandering, condemning, and proscribing my New Testament when it appeared under my name, only to make it required reading when it appeared under someone else's. But what sort of virtue it takes to slur and slander someone else's book, and then steal it and put it out under one's own name, using said slandered work to seek praise and renown for oneself – that is a question I leave it to his Judge to determine. Meanwhile I'm pleased and satisfied that my hard work – and this was also St Paul's boast – is certain to be promoted by my opponents too, and that Luther's book will be read, not under his own name, but under that of his enemies. Could revenge be any sweeter?

But to return to the matter at hand – since your papist wishes to make such a fuss about the word 'sola' ('alone'), go straight back to him and say, "Dr Martin Luther wishes to keep it as it is, and says that a papist and a donkey are one and the same." *Sic volo, sic iubeo, sit pro ratione voluntas*[26] - we do not wish to be the papists' pupils or disciples, but their masters and judges. And this time we will outstrut and outbrag those donkey-heads, and just as St Paul matched the religious lunatics of his age boast for boast, so will I with the donkeys of mine. Are they doctors of theology? So am I. Are they scholars? So am I. Are they preachers? So am I. Are they theologians? So am I. Are they debaters? So am I. Are they philosophers? So am I. Are they logicians?

---

[26] 'I desire it; I command it; may my will be reason enough'. This is a quotation from the Roman satirist Juvenal (*Satire VI*, line 223).

Ich auch. Sie sind Legenten? Ich auch. Sie schreiben buͤcher? Ich auch.

Vnd wil weiter rhuͤmen: Ich kan Psalmen vnd Prophetē außlegen / Das kuͤnnen sie nicht. Ich kan dolmetzschen / Dz koͤnnen sie nicht. Ich kan die heiligen schrifft lesen / Das koͤnnen sie nicht. Ich kan biten / Das koͤnnen sie nicht. Vnd das ich herunter kome / Ich kan yhr eygen Dialectica vnd Philosophia bas / denn sie selbs allesampt. Vnd weiß dazu fur war / das yhr keiner yhren Aristotelem verstehet. Vnnd ist einer vnter yn allen der ein proemium odder Capittel ym Aristotele recht verstehet / so wil ich mich lassen prellen. Ich rede ytzt nicht zuuil / den̄ ich bin durch yhre kunst alle erzogen vnd erfaren von jugent auff / weiß fast wol wie tieff vnd weit sie ist. So wissen sie auch wol / das ichs alles weiß vnd kan / was sie koͤnnen / Noch handeln die heillosen leute gegen mir / als were ich ein gast jnn yhrer kunst / der aller erst heut morgen komen were / vn̄ noch nie weder gesehen noch gehoͤrt hette / was sie leren odder koͤnnen / So gar herrlich prangen sie herein mit yhrer kunst / vnd leren mich / was ich vor zwentzig jaren an den schuhen zu rissen habe / das ich auch mit jhener metzen auff all yhr plerren vnd schreien singen mus / Ich habs fur siben jaren gewist / das hůffnegel eysen sind.

Das sey auff ewr erste Frag geantwortet / vn̄ bitte euch / woͤllet solchen Eseln ja nicht anders noch mehr antworten auff yhr vnnuͤtze geplerre vom wort Sola / Denn also viel / Luther wils so haben / vn̄ spricht / Er sey ein Doctor vber alle Doctor jm gantzen Bapstum / da sols bey bleiben /

So am I. Do they give lectures? So do I. Do they write books? So do I.

And I haven't finished boasting: I can interpret the Psalms and the Prophets – they can't. I can translate – they can't. I can read Holy Scripture – they can't. I can pray – they can't. And coming down to basics, I know their dialectic and philosophy better than the lot of them put together.[27] What's more, I know for a fact that not one of them understands their Aristotle: if there's a single one among all of them who properly grasps one preface or chapter in Aristotle, I'll be hanged![28] I'm not exaggerating, because I am trained in – and have practised – every one of their arts since childhood, and I am well aware how profound and far-reaching they are. And they are well aware that I know it all and can do anything they can do. Yet these God-forsaken people treat me like a stranger to their arts, like someone who turned up for the first time this morning, never having seen, or even heard about, what they teach or what they know. They flaunt their learning in such a high-handed way, lecturing me on what I cut my teeth on twenty years ago,[29] that, in the face of all their screaming and shouting, I'm compelled to join in with that girl who chanted, 'Don't try teaching grandmother to suck eggs'.[30]

Let that be the answer to your first question, and please give no further response to those donkeys and their pointless fuss about the word 'sola' than simply this: "Luther wishes to keep it as it is, and says that he is a doctor of theology above all others throughout the papacy," and that's that.

---

[27] By 'basics', Luther is referring to the liberal arts, which included branches of philosophy, as opposed to the higher disciplines of theology and law.

[28] Literally: 'I'm willing to be tossed (in the air)'.

[29] Literally: 'what I tore to pieces on my shoes twenty years ago'.

[30] Literally: 'I have known for seven years that horseshoe nails are made of iron'.

Ich will sie hinfürt schlecht verachten vnd veracht haben / so lange sie solche leute (ich wolt sagen) Esel sind / Denn es sind solche vnuerschempte tropffen vnter yhn / die auch yhr eigen der Sophisten kunst nye gelernt haben / wie Doctor Schmidt / vnd doctor Rotzlöffel / vnd seine gleichen / vnd legen sich gleich wol widder mich / yn dieser sachen / die nicht allein vber die sophisterey / sondern auch (wie sanct Paulus sagt) vber aller welt weißheit vnd vernunfft ist.[31] Zwar es durfft ein Esel nicht viel singen / man kennet yn sonst wol bey den ohrē.

Euch aber vnd den vnsern wil ich anzeigen / warumb ich dz wort (sola) hab wöllen brauchen / Wiewol Roma. 3.[32] nicht sola / sondern solum odder tantum von mir gebraucht ist. Also fein sehen die Esel meinen text an. Aber doch hab ichs sonst anders wo sola fide gebraucht vñ wil auch beide solum vnd sola haben. Ich hab mich des geflissen ym dolmetzschen / das ich rein vnd klar teutsch geben möchte. Vnd ist vns wol offt begegnet / das wir viertzehen tage / drey / vier wochen haben ein einiges wort gesůcht vnd gefragt / habens dennoch zu weilen nicht funden. Im Hiob erbeiten wir also / M. Philips / Aurogallus vnd ich / das wir yn vier tagen zu weilen kaum drey zeilen kundten fertigen. Lieber / nu es verdeutscht vñ bereit ist / kans ein yeder lesen vnd meistern / Laufft einer ytzt mit den augen durch drey vier bletter vnd stost nicht ein mal an / wird aber nicht gewar welche wacken und klötze da gelegen sind / da er ytzt vber hin gehet / wie vber ein gehoffelt bret / da wir haben můssen schwitzen vñ vns engsten / ehe den wir solche wacken vnd klotze aus dem wege reümeten / auff das man kůndte so fein daher gehen. Es ist gut pflugen / wenn der acker gereinigt ist. Aber den wald vnd die stöcke aus rotten / vnd dē acker zu richten / da will niemandt an. Es ist bey der welt kein danck zu verdienen /

---

[31] 1 Corinthians 1: 19–21.

[32] Romans 3: 28. Luther's German translation is: 'Wir halten / das der mensch gerecht werde on des gesetzs werck / allein durch den glauben'.

From now on I'm just going to ignore them and make sure they're ignored for as long as they are the sort of people (or rather donkeys) that they are. Don't forget, they include a number of shameless idiots who have never even mastered their own art of sophistry, such as Dr. Smith and Dr. Snotty-Nose[33] and others like him, and yet they inveigh against me on this matter, which not only goes beyond sophistry, but also, as Saint Paul writes, transcends all the wisdom and understanding in the world. The fact is, a donkey doesn't need to do much braying: you just have to look at his ears.

But for you and our own people I'll explain why I chose to use the word 'sola' – even though in Romans 3 it wasn't 'sola', but 'solum' or 'tantum' that I used. See how carefully those donkeys study what I wrote![34] Still, I've put 'sola fide' elsewhere,[35] and I want to keep both 'solum' and 'sola'. I've worked hard to produce a translation in crisp and clear German. We've very often spent two, three, four weeks looking for a single word, making inquiries, and sometimes still not found it. When we were translating the Book of Job, there were times when Melanchthon, Aurogallus, and I barely managed three lines in four days. But my friend, now that the German version is ready, anyone can read and opine on it. You can cast your eye over three or four pages without tripping up once, not realising what lumps of stone and clods of earth there used to be where you're now walking as if on smoothly planed timber – we had to toil and struggle to clear those stones and clods out of the way for people to walk along so easily. Ploughing is easy when the field has been cleaned up, but digging out the bits of wood and the tree-stumps and preparing the field is a job no-one wants. The world isn't grateful for this.

---

[33] Johann Faber and Johann Dobeneck; see Glossary of Names.

[34] The Latin words 'sola', 'solum', and 'tantum' all mean 'only, alone', but 'sola' is an adjective, while 'solum' and 'tantum' are adverbs. Luther's use of 'alone' in Romans 3: 28 is adverbial.

[35] For example, in Luther's preface to his translation of Romans in 1529.

Kan doch Got selbs mit der sonnen / ja mit himel vnd erden / noch mit seines eigen sons tod keinen danck verdienen / sie sey vn̄ bleibt welt deß teuffels namen / weil sie ja nicht anders will.

Also habe ich hie Roma. 3. fast wol gewist / das ym Lateinischen vnd krigischen text das wort (solum) nicht stehet / vnd hettē mich solchs die papisten nicht dürffen leren. War ists. Dise vier buchstaben s o l a stehen nicht drinnen / welche buchstaben die Eselskópff ansehen / wie die kue ein new thor / Sehen aber nicht das gleichwol die meinung des text ynn sich hat / vnd wo mans wil klar vnd gewaltiglich verteutschen / so gehoret es hinein / den̄ ich habe deutsch / nicht lateinisch noch kriegisch reden wóllen / da ich teutsch zu reden ym dolmetzschen furgenomen hatte. Das ist aber die art vnser deutschen sprache / wenn sie ein rede begibt / von zweyen dingen / der man eins bekennet / vn̄ das ander verneinet / so braucht man des worts solum (allein) neben dem wort (nicht oder kein) / Als wenn man sagt / Der Baür bringt allein korn vn̄ kein geldt / Nein / ich hab warlich ytzt nicht geldt /sondern allein korn. Ich hab allein gessen vnd noch nicht getruncken. Hastu allein geschrieben vnd nicht vberlesen? Vnd der gleichen vnzeliche weise yn teglichen brauch.

In disen reden allē / obs gleich die lateinische oder kriechische sprach nicht thut / so thuts doch die deutsche / vnd ist yhr art / das sie das Wort (allein) hinzu setzt / auff das das wort (nicht odder kein) deste volliger vnd deutlicher sey / Denn wie wol ich auch sage / Der Baür bringt korn vn̄ kein geld / So laut doch das wort (kein geldt) nicht so vollig vnd deutlich / als wenn ich sage / Der Baür bringt allein korn vnd kein geldt / vnd hilfft hie das wort (Allein) dem wort (kein) so viel / das es ein vollige Deutsche klare rede wird / den man mus nicht die buchstaben inn der lateinischē sprachen fragē / wie man sol Deutsch redē / wie diese esel thun / sondern / man mus die mutter jhm hause / die kinder auff der gassen / den gemeinen mā auff dem marckt drumb fragen / vn̄ den selbigē auff das maul sehen / wie sie reden / vnd darnach dolmetzschen / so verstehen sie es den / vn̄ mercken / das man Deutsch mit jn redet.

For that matter, the world isn't grateful to God for what he has given – the sun, heaven and earth of course, even the death of His own Son. The world can stay as it is, by devil, since it actually doesn't want to change.

So here in Romans Chapter 3, I was fully aware that the word 'solum' doesn't occur in the Latin or Greek text and didn't need the papists to teach me that. It's true: these four letters *s-o-l-a* are not there – these four letters that the donkey-heads are gawping at like cows at a new gate. But they don't see that this actually captures the meaning of the text, and if you're going for a clear and vigorous German version, the word belongs here – after all, I was aiming for something that sounded German, not Latin or Greek, given that it was a German translation I'd set out to produce. That's what you do in German when making a statement about two things, one of which is affirmed and the other denied – you use the word 'solum' ('only' or 'alone') along with the word 'not' or 'no'. This is the case when you say, 'The farmer brings only grain and no money', 'No, I've really got no money at the moment, but only grain', 'I've only eaten and not drunk', 'Have you only written it down and not read it through?' – and countless similar expressions in everyday use.

In all these phrases, although Latin and Greek don't do this, German does, and it's natural in German to add the word 'only' to bring out the meaning of the word 'not' or 'no' all the more fully and clearly. It's true that I can also say, 'The farmer brings grain and no money', but the words 'no money' don't make it as complete and clear as when I say, 'The farmer brings only grain and no money'. Here the word 'only' supports the word 'no' to create a clear, genuinely German phrase. We mustn't consult the Latin text about how to speak German, as these donkeys do, but we must consult the mother at home, children in the street, and the ordinary man in the market-place, watch them mouth their words, and translate accordingly. That way they'll understand, and see that they're being spoken to in German.

Als wenn Christus spricht / Ex abundantia cordis os loquitur.[36] Wenn ich den Eseln sol folgen / die werden mir die buchstaben furlegen / vnd also dolmetzschen / Auß dem vberflus des hertzen redet der mund. Sage mir / Ist das deutsch geredt? Welcher deutscher verstehet solchs? Was ist vberflus des hertzē fur ein ding? Das kan kein deutscher sagen / Er wolt denn sagen / es sey das einer allzu ein gros hertz habe / oder zu vil hertzes habe / wie wol das auch noch nicht recht ist / deñ vberflus des hertzen ist kein deutsch / so wenig / als das deutsch ist / Vberflus des hauses / vberflus des kacheloffens / vberflus der banck / sondern also redet die můtter ym haus vnd der gemeine man / Wes das hertz vol ist / des gehet der mund vber / dz heist gut deutsch geredt / des ich mich geflissen / vñ leider nicht allwege erreicht noch troffen habe / Deñ die lateinischē buchstabē hindern aus der massen seer gut deutsch zu reden.

Also / weñ der verrether Judas sagt / Matthei 26: Vt quid perditio hec? Vnd Marci 14. Vt quid perditio ista vngenti facta est? Folge ich den Eseln vnd buchstabilisten / so mus ichs also verdeutschen: Warumb ist dise verlierung der salben geschehen? Was ist aber das fur deutsch? Welcher deutscher redet also / verlierung der salben ist geschehen? Vnd wenn ers wol verstehet / so denckt er / die salbe sey verloren / vnd musse sie etwa wider suchen / Wiewol das auch noch tunckel vnd vngewiß lautet. Wenn nu das gut deutsch ist / warumb tretten sie nicht erfur / vñ machen vns ein solch fein hubsch new deutsch Testament / vñ lassen des Luthers Testament ligen? Ich meine ja sie solten yhre kunst an den tag bringen / Aber der deutsche man redet also / Vt quid &c.: Was sol doch solcher vnrat? odder / was sol doch solcher schade? Nein / Es ist schade vmb die salbe / das ist gut deutsch / daraus man verstehet / das Magdalene mit der verschutten salben sey vnrethlich vmbgangen vnd habe schadenn gethan / das war Judas meinung / denn er gedacht bessern rat damit zu schaffen.

---

[36] Matthew 12: 34 and Luke 6: 45.

So, when Christ says, 'Ex abundantia cordis os loquitur', if I'm to follow the donkeys, I'll have to take the exact wording they put in front of me and translate as follows: 'Out of the abundance of heart the mouth speaks'. Tell me, does that sound German? Does any German speaker understand a phrase like that? What sort of thing is 'abundance of heart'? No German says that, unless they mean that someone is too great-hearted or has too much heart, although even that still isn't right: 'abundance of heart' is no more German than 'abundance of house', 'abundance of stove', 'abundance of bench'. But your mother at home and the man in the street say, 'What fills the heart, pours from the lips'. That's what I call good German, which I've tried hard to achieve, and unfortunately not always got there and hit the mark, because the Latin wording is an enormous obstacle to making the German sound really good.

Likewise, when Judas the traitor says in Matthew 26: 8, 'Ut quid perditio haec?' and in Mark 14: 4, 'Ut quid perditio ista unguenti facta est?' - if I follow those donkeys and text-maniacs, I will have to render this into German as follows: 'Why has this loss of ointment occurred?' But what sort of German is that? Does any German say, 'Loss of ointment has occurred'? Even if they understand it, they'll think that the ointment has got lost and has to be found again, although even that still sounds obscure and unclear. Well, if that's good German, why don't they come out and produce a fine, charming, new German Testament like that for us, and leave Luther's Testament well alone? What I really mean is that they should display their talent for all to see. But for 'Ut quid, etc', a German would say, 'Why such waste?' or, 'Why such extravagance?' or, 'Don't waste the ointment.' That is good German, which makes it clear that Mary Magdalene[37] was wrong to pour out the ointment and wasted it, which was what Judas meant, because he thought he could have made better use of it.

---

[37] The woman in the house of Simon the leper is not named in the New Testament, but was traditionally taken to be Mary Magdalene.

Item da der Engel Mariam grůsset vnd spricht: Gegrůsset seistu / Maria vol gnadē / der Herr mit dir?[38] Wolan / so ists biß her / schlecht den lateinischen buchstaben nach verdeutschet / sage mir aber ob solchs auch gut deutsch sey? Wo redet der deutsch man also / du bist vol gnaden? Vnd welcher Deutscher verstehet / was gsagt sey / vol gnaden? Er mus dencken an ein vas vol bier / oder beutel vol geldes / darumb hab ichs vordeutscht. Du holdselige / da mit doch ein Deutscher / dester meher hin zu kan dencken / was der engel meinet mit seinem grus. Aber hie wőllen die Papisten toll werden vber mich / das ich den Engelischen grus verderbet habe. Wie wol ich dennoch da mit nicht das beste deutsch habe troffen. Vnd hette ich das beste deutsch hie sollen nemen / vnd den grus also verdeutschen / Gott grusse dich du liebe Maria (denn so vil wil der Engel sagen / vnd so wurde er geredt haben / wan er hette wollen sie deutsch grussen) ich halt sie solten sich wol selbs erhenckt haben fur grosser andacht / zu der lieben Maria / das ich den grus so zu nichte gemacht hette.

Aber was frage ich darnach? sie toben oder rasen / jch wil nicht wehren / das sie verdeutschen was sie wőllen / ich wil aber auch verdeutschē / nicht wie sie wőllen / sonder wie ich wil / wer es nicht haben wil / der las mirs stehen / vñ halt seine meisterschafft bey sich / denn ich wil ir weder sehen noch hőren / sie dorffen fur mein dolmetzschen nicht antwort geben / noch rechenschafft thun / Das hőrestu wol / ich wil sagen / du holdselige Maria / du liebe Maria. vnd las sie sagen / du volgnaden Maria. Wer Deutsch kan / der weis wol / welch ein hertzlich fein wort das ist / die liebe Maria / der lieb Gott / der liebe Keiser / der liebe fürst / der lieb man / das liebe kind.

---

[38] Luke 1: 28.

And what about when the angel greets Mary and says, 'Hail Mary, full of grace, the Lord is with you'?[39] Well, in the past this has just been rendered word for word into German from the Latin, but tell me – seriously – is this good German? Show me any German who says, 'You are full of grace'. For that matter, what German will understand the meaning of 'full of grace'? They're going to think of a barrel full of beer or a bag full of money. That's why I rendered it into German as 'gracious one', to make it easier for a German to actually work out what the angel means by his greeting. But here the papists choose to throw a fit on the grounds that I have corrupted the angelic greeting – although even with this wording I still didn't get the German exactly right. If I had got the German exactly right here and rendered the greeting as, 'God be with you, dear Mary' (which is, after all, what the angel means, and how he would have spoken if he'd wanted to greet her in German), I'm convinced they would have positively hanged themselves in their fanatical devotion to dear Mary on the grounds that I had destroyed the greeting.

But what do I care? They can rant and rave, and I'm not going to stop them from rendering into German whatever they want, but I'm going to use German too, and not as they want, but as I do. If people don't like it, they should leave it alone and keep their genius to themselves – I will neither look at nor listen to any of it. Nor do they need to answer for my translation or take responsibility for it. Now listen – I will go on saying, 'gracious Mary' and, 'dear Mary', and they can go on saying, 'full-of-grace Mary'. People who can speak German know what a fine, heartfelt word 'dear' is, as in 'dear Mary', 'dear God', 'dear emperor', 'dear prince', 'dear man', 'dear child'.

---

[39] Luke 1: 28 (the Angelic Salutation); the Vulgate here reads, 'Ave, gratia plena, Dominus tecum', literally 'Hail, woman full of grace, the Lord with you'. For the meaning of 'grace' in Luther's theology and a discussion of Luther's translation here, see Background, Sections 3 and 4.

Vnd ich weis nicht / ob man das wort liebe / auch so hertzlich vnd gnugsam in Lateinischer oder andern sprachen reden muͤg / das also dringe vnd klinge ynns hertz / durch alle sinne wie es thut in vnser sprache.

Denn ich halt S. Lucas als ein meister in Hebreischer vnd Greckischer sprache / hab das Hebreisch wort / so der Engel gebraucht / woͤllen mit dem Greckischen kecharitomeni / treffen vnd deutlich geben. Vnd denck mir der Engel Gabriel habe mit Maria geredt / wie er mit Daniel redet / vnd nennet jnn / Hamudoth vñ Isch Hamudoth / vir desideriorum / das ist / du lieber Daniel. Denn das ist Gabrielis weise zu reden / wie wir jhm Daniel sehen.[40] Wenn ich nu den buchstaben nach / aus der esel kunst / solt des Engels wort verdeutschen / muste ich also sagen / Daniel du man der begirungen oder / Daniel du man der luͤste / O das were schon deutsch / Ein deutscher horet wol / das Man / Luͤste / oder begyrunge / deutsche wort sind / wie wol es nicht eytel reine deutsche wort sind / sondern lust vnd begyr / weren wol besser. Aber wenn sie so zusamen gefasset werden / du man der begyrungen / so weiß kein deutscher was gesagt ist / denckt / das Daniel villeicht vol boͤser lust stecke / Das hiesse denn fein gedolmetzscht. Darumb mus ich hie die buchstaben faren lassen / vnnd forschen / wie der Deutsche man solchs redet / welchs der Ebreische mā isch Hamudoth redet / So finde ich / das der deutsche mā also spricht / Du lieber Daniel / du liebe Maria / oder du holdselige mad / du medliche junckfraw / du zartes weib / vnd der gleichen. Deñ wer dolmetzschen wil / mus grosse vorrath von worten haben / das er die wol koͤnne haben / wo eins an allen orten nicht lauten will.

[40] Daniel 9: 23, 10: 11, and 10: 19.

I'm not sure whether Latin or any other language can express 'dear' in such a heartfelt and satisfying way, resonating through all the senses and going straight to the heart, as the word 'dear' does in our language.

I believe that St Luke, who was a master of Hebrew and Greek, wanted to capture and clearly convey with 'kecharitomene'[41] the sense of the Hebrew word used by the angel. And I think that the angel Gabriel spoke to Mary as he speaks to Daniel when he calls him 'Chamudot' and 'Ish Chamudot' (*vir desideriorum*),[42] that is, 'dear Daniel'. That's how the angel Gabriel speaks, as we can see in the book of Daniel. Now, if I were going to put the angel's words into German word for word, using the donkeys' technique, I'd have to say, 'Daniel, you man of desires' or, 'Daniel, you man of lusts'. Oh, that would be charming German! Of course, a German recognizes 'man', 'lusts', and 'desires' as German words when he hears them (although these are not the most natural German words to use: 'desire' and 'lust' would really be better). But when the words are combined as 'you man of desires', no German will know what's being said, and will think that Daniel is perhaps full of sinful desire. What fine translating that would be! That's why I have to depart from the exact wording here and try to find out what a German says when a Hebrew says, 'Ish Chamudot'. And I discover that a German says, 'dear Daniel', 'dear Mary', or 'gracious maiden', 'lovely young lady', 'sweet woman', and so on. A translator needs a large supply of words to hand in case one of them doesn't sound right everywhere.

---

[41] This Greek word means 'beloved, endowed with favour/grace'.

[42] The Latin means literally 'man of desires'.

Vnd was sol ich vil vnd lange sagen von dolmetzschenn? Solt ich aller meiner wort vrsachen vnnd gedancken anzeigen / ich muͤste wol ein jar dran zu schreiben haben. Was dolmetschen fur kunst vnd erbeit sey / das hab ich wol erfaren / darumb wil ich keinen papstesel noch maulesel / die nichts versucht habē / hierinn zum richter oder thadeller leiden. Wer mein dolmetzschen nicht wil / der las es anstehen / Der Teuffel dancke yhm / wers vngerne hat oder on meinen willen vnd wissen meistert. Sols gemeistert werden / so wil ichs selber thun. Wo ichs selber nicht thu / da lasse man mir mein dolmetzschen mit friden / vnd mache ein iglicher was er wil fur sich selbs / vnd habe ym ein gut jar.

Das kan ich mit gutem gewissen zeugen / das ich meine hoͤchste trew vnd vleiß drinnen erzeigt / vnd nye kein falsche gedanckē gehabt habe / denn ich habe keinen heller da fur genomen noch gesuͤcht / noch damit gewonnen / So hab ich meine ehre drinnē nicht gemeinet / das weis Gott mein Herr / sondern habs zu dienst gethan den lieben Christen / vnnd zu ehren einem der droben sitzet / der mir alle stunde so vil guts thut / das wenn ich tausent mal so vil vnd vleissig gedolmetzscht / dennoch nicht eine stunde verdienet hette zu leben / odder ein gesundt auge zu haben / Es ist alles seiner gnaden vñ barmhertzigkeit / was ich bin vnd habe / Ja es ist seines theurē bluts und saüren schweißes / darumb sols auch (ob Gott wil) alles yhm zu ehren dienen / mit freuden vnnd von hertzen. Lestern mich die Sudeler vnd Bapstesel / wol an / so lobenn mich die frumen Christen sampt yhrem hern Christo / Vnd bin allzu reichlich belohnet / wo mich nůr ein einiger Christ fur einen trewē erbeiter erkennet. Ich frag nach Bapsteseln nichts / sie sind nicht werd / das sie meine erbeit sollen erkennen / vnd solt mir ym grund meins hertzen leid sein / das sie mich lobetenn. Ihr lestern ist mein hoͤhester rhům vñ ehr /

But why keep on about translating? If I were going to point out the reason for every word I use and the thinking behind it, it'd take me a good year to put it in writing. The art and effort of translating is something I've actually experienced, which is why I can do without having my work judged and criticized by the donkeys of popedom and braying mules who've never tried their hand at it. People who don't like my translating should leave it be. If they disapprove of it or criticize it without my consent or knowledge, they can look to the devil for thanks. If someone has to criticize it, it will be me, and if I don't, then kindly leave me and my translation in peace. Each to his own, and good riddance!

This I can declare with a clear conscience: I've worked on this with the utmost effort and devotion, and never, ever with an ulterior motive. I haven't received or requested a penny for it nor earned one from it. And, as the Lord God is my witness, I didn't do it for my own glory, but as a service to my fellow Christians and for the glory of One who sits on high and blesses me so much every hour that, even if I'd translated a thousand times as much and as diligently, I wouldn't have deserved to breathe and behold the world for a single hour.[43] Everything I am and everything I have is down to his grace and mercy, and, what's more, to his precious blood and bitter sweat, which is also why, God willing, everything should be done – joyfully and sincerely – for His glory. Oh yes, the bunglers and donkeys of popedom may well slander me, but righteous Christians, including Christ their Lord, praise me. And I am more than amply rewarded if even a single Christian acknowledges me as a faithful worker. I couldn't care less about the donkeys of popedom: they aren't worthy even to acknowledge my work, and I would find it deeply annoying if they did compliment me: for me their insults are the highest praise and honour.

---

[43] Literally: 'I would not have deserved to live for one hour or to have a healthy eye'.

Ich will doch ein Doctor / ja auch ein ausbuͤndiger Doctor sein / vnd sie sollen mir den namen nicht nemen / biß an den Juͤngsten tag / das weiß ich furwar.

Doch hab ich widerumb nicht allzu frey die buchstaben lassen faren / Sondern mit grossen sorgen sampt meinen gehülffen drauff gesehen / das wo etwa an einem ort gelegenn ist / hab ichs nach den buchstaben behalten / vñ bin nicht so frey dauon gangē / als Johannes .6.[44] da Christus spricht / Disen hat Got der vatter versiegelt / da were wol besser deutsch gewest / Disen hat Gott d' Vater gezeichent / odd' disen meinet Gott der vater. Aber ich habe ehe woͤllen der deutschen sprache abbrechen / denn von dem wort weichen. Ah es ist dolmetzschen ja nicht eines iglichen kunst / wie die tollen Heiligē meinē / Es gehoͤret dazu ein recht / frum / trew / vleissig / forchtsam / Christlich / geleret / erfarn / geuͤbet hertz / Darumb halt ich / das kein falscher Christ noch rottengeist trewlich dolmetzschen koͤnne / wie das wol scheinet inn den prophetenn zu Wormbs verdeutschet / darinn doch warlich grosser vleis geschehen / vnd meinem deutschen fast nach gangen ist.

[44] John 6: 27.

But I'll carry on being a doctor of theology – yes, and a distinguished one – a title they shan't take away from me until the Day of Judgement; that much I know for certain.

On the other hand I haven't taken too many liberties with the text, but wherever the meaning turns on a precise point I have, along with my assistants, taken great care to keep close to the text and not to stray so far from it. For example, in John 6: 27, where Christ says, 'This is the man whom God the Father has sealed', it would certainly have been better German to say, 'This is the man whom God the Father has indicated' or, 'This is the man whom God the Father means'. But I would rather force the German language than stray from the word.[45] Look, translation isn't something just anyone can do, as those religious lunatics imagine. It requires a devout, righteous, true, diligent, God-fearing, Christian, learned, educated, experienced heart. This is why I consider it impossible for someone who is not a true Christian or for a factionalist to be a faithful translator. This is clear from the German version of the Prophets which was carried out at Worms, although it was a really meticulous piece of work which came very close to my own German.

[45] On Luther's defence of word for word translation here, see Background, Section 4.

Aber es sind Jůden da bey gewest / die Christo nicht grosse hulde erzeigt haben / sonst were kunst vnd vleiß genug da.

Das sey vom dolmetzschen vñ art der sprachen gesagt. Aber nu hab ich nicht allein der sprachen art vertrawet vnd gefolget / das ich Roma. 3. solum (Allein) hab hinzu gesetzt / Sonder der text vnd die meinung S. Pauli foddern vnd erzwingens mit gewallt / denn er handelt ja daselbs das hauptstůck Christlicher lere / nemlich das wir durch den glauben an Christū / on alle werck des gesetzs gerecht werden / Vnd schneit alle werck so rein abe / dz er auch spricht / des gesetzes (das doch Gottes gesetz vñ wort ist) werck nicht helffen zur gerechtigkeit / Vnd setzt zum exempel Abraham / das der selbige sey so gar on werck gerecht worden / das auch das hȯhest werck / das dazu mal new gepotē ward von got fur vnd vber allen andern gesetzen vnd wercken / nemlich die beschneidung / yhm nicht geholffen hab zur gerechtigkeit / sonder sey on die beschneidung vnd on alle werck gerecht worden durch den glaubē wie er spricht Cap. 4. Ist Abraham durch werck gerecht wordenn / so mag er sich rhůmen / aber nicht fur Gott. Wo man aber alle werck so rein abschneit / vñ da mus ja die meinung sein / das allein der glaube gerecht mache / vnd wer deutlich vnd durre von solchem abschneiden der werck redet wil / der mus sagen / Allein der glaube / vnd nicht die werck machen vns gerecht / dz zwinget die sache selbs neben der sprachen art.

But there were Jews involved in it who were not very favourably inclined towards Christ – apart from that it was skilfully and carefully enough done.[46]

That's enough about translating and the art of language. But it wasn't just a reliance on the art of language that led me to add the word 'solum' ('only') in Romans 3: rather, the text itself and St Paul's meaning positively demand and require it. For it is precisely here that he deals with the central tenet of Christian teaching, namely that we are justified through faith in Christ without any works of the law. And St Paul so entirely excludes works that he even says that the works of the law – God's law and God's word, in fact - do not help us to justification. He cites the example of Abraham who, he says, was justified so entirely to the exclusion of works that even the supreme work, which had in fact only just been ordained by God over and above all other laws and works, namely circumcision, did not help him to justification. Instead he was justified, without circumcision and without any works, through faith, as St Paul says in chapter 4: 2: 'If Abraham was justified through works, he may boast of it, but not before God.' Now if all works are so entirely excluded, the meaning must indeed be that only faith justifies, and anyone who wants to talk about the exclusion of works in plain and simple language will have to say, 'Only faith justifies us, and not works'. This is required by the subject matter itself as well as by the art of language.

---

[46] This refers to the translation of the Prophets from the Hebrew by Ludwig Hätzer and Hans Denck, published at Worms in 1527. Hätzer and Denck were Anabaptists (believers in adult, not infant, baptism) and anti-trinitarians. Hätzer even denied the divinity of Christ, and Luther may have had him in mind when he claims that Jews were involved in this translation. Luther was working on his German version of the Prophets at the time he wrote the *Sendbrief*.

Ja sprechen sie / Es laut ergerlich / vnd die leute lernē daraus verstehen / das sie keine gute werck thun duͤrffen. Lieber was sol man sagen? Ists nicht viel ergerlicher / das S. Pauls selbs nicht sagt / allein der glaube / sondern schuttets wol groͤber eraus / vnd stosset dem faß den boden aus vnd spricht / On des gesetzs werck / Vnd Gala. 1. nicht durch die werck des gesetzes / vñ des vil mehr an andern orten / denn das wort (allein der glaube) moͤcht noch eine gloß findē / Aber das wort (on werck des gesetzs) ist so grob / ergerlich / schendtlich / das man mit keiner glossenn helffen kan / Wie viel mehr moͤchten hieraus die leute lernen kein gute werck thun / da sie hoͤren mit so durren starcken worten von den werckē selbs predigen (Kein werck / on werck / nicht durch werck) / ist nu dz nicht ergerlich / das mā (on werck / kein werck / nicht durch werck) predigt / was solts deñ ergerlich sein / so man diß (allein der glaube) predigt?

Vnd dz noch ergerlich ist / S. Paulus verwuͤrfft nicht schlechte gemeine werck / sonder des gesetzes selbs. Daraus moͤchte wol yemand sich noch mehr ergern vnd sagen / Das gesetz sey verdāpt vnd verflucht fur Gott / vnd man solle eytel boses thun / wie die theten Roman. 3: Last vns boͤses thun / auff das es gut werde / wie auch ein rotten geyst zu vnser zeit anfieng. Solt man vmb solcher ergernis willen S. Paulus wort verlaugnen / oder nicht frisch vnd frey vom glauben reden?

They will claim that this sounds alarming and that people will understand it to mean that they do not need to do good works. Really, my friend, what can one say? Isn't it much more alarming that St Paul himself, rather than saying 'faith alone', is far more blatant about it, and completely opens the floodgates[47] by using the words 'without the works of the law', and 'not by the works of the law' in Galatians 2: 16 and a good many other places as well? For the phrase 'faith alone' could give rise to a different interpretation, but the words 'without the works of the law' are so blatant, alarming, offensive that no amount of interpretation can help. How much more might people learn from this 'not to do good works', when they hear preaching about the works themselves with such simple and stark phrases as 'no works', 'without works', 'not through works'! So if it isn't alarming to preach 'without works', 'no works', 'not through works', why should it be alarming to preach 'faith alone'?

What's more alarming still is that St Paul rejects not simple, ordinary works but 'works of the law'. One could easily be even more alarmed by this and say that here the law is being condemned and cursed before God, and we're being told to do nothing but evil, like those people in Romans 3: 8 who said, 'Let us do evil, so that good may come of it' - which is also what one factional spirit took to saying in our own age.[48] Are we meant to deny St Paul's words on the grounds that they are alarming, or not talk freely and frankly about faith?

---

[47] Literally: 'knock the bottom out of the barrel'.

[48] Luther may be referring here to Thomas Müntzer, a radical Reformation preacher and leader of the peasants' uprising of 1524-5, which Luther opposed. Müntzer was captured and executed after the Battle of Frankenhausen in May 1525. Luther often used 'Rottengeist' ('factionalist') to refer to Müntzer.

Lieber eben S. Paulus vñ wir wͤllen solch ergernis haben / vñ leren vmb keiner ander vrsachen willen / so starck wider die werck / vñ treiben allein auff den glauben / das die leute sollen sich ergern / stossen vnd fallen / damit sie mugen lernen vñ wissen / das sie durch yr gute werck nit frum werden / sondern allein durch Christus tod vñ aufferstehē / Kͤnnen sie nu durch gute werck des gesetzes nicht frum werden / wie vil weniger werden sie frum werden durch bͤse werck vñ on gesetz / Darumb folget es nicht / Gute werck helffen nicht / darumb helffen bͤse werck / gleich als nicht fein folgt / Die sonne kan dem blinden nicht helffen das er sehe / darumb mus ym die nacht vnd finsternis helffen / das er sehe.

Mich wundert aber / das man sich yn diser offentlichen sachē so mag sperrē. Sage mir doch / ob Christus tod vñ aufferste ē vnser werck sey / das wir thun / oder nicht? Es ist ja nit vnser werck / noch einiges gesetzes werck. Nu macht vns ja allein Christus tod vñ aufferstehen frey von sunden vñ frum / wie Paulus sagt Ro. 4. Er ist gestorbē vmb vnser sunde willen / vñ auffer standē vmb vnser gerechtigkeit willē. Weiter sage mir / Welchs ist dz werck / damit wir Christus tod vñ aufferstehē fassen vñ haltē? Es mus ja kein eusserlich werck / sondern allein der ewige glaube ym hertzen sein / der selbige allein / ja gar allein / vnd on alle werck fasset solchen tod vñ aufferstehen wo es gepredigt wird durchs Euangelion. Was ists deñ nu / dz man so tobet vñ wͤtet / ketzert vñ brēnet / so die sach ym grundt selbs klerlich da ligt und beweiset / das allein der glaube Christus tod vñ aufferstehē fasse on alle werck / vnd der selbige tod vñ aufferstehen sey vnser leben vnd gerechtigkeit. So es deñ an ym selbs offentlich also ist / dz allein der glaube vns solch lebē vñ gerechtigkeit bringet / fasset vñ gibt / Warūb soll man deñ nicht auch also redē? Es ist nit ketzerey / dz der glaube allein Christū fasset / vñ das leben gibt / Aber ketzerey muss es sein wer solchs sagt odʼ redet.

In fact, my friend, St Paul and we are trying to be alarming, and the only reason why we're teaching so forcefully against works and insisting exclusively on faith is to alarm people, to trip them up, and jolt them into acknowledging that they cannot become righteous[49] through their good works, but only through Christ's death and resurrection. Given that they cannot become righteous through the good works of the law, how much less will they become righteous through evil works and without the law! So it doesn't follow from the fact that good works don't help that bad works do, just as it doesn't follow necessarily from the fact that the sun can't help a blind man to see that night and darkness do.

But I'm amazed that people can baulk like this at something so obvious. Just tell me: is Christ's death and resurrection our work, which we do, or not? No, it is not our work, nor the work of any law. It is Christ's death and resurrection alone which frees us from sin and makes us righteous, as Paul says in Romans 4: 25: 'He died for our sins and rose for our justification'. And tell me this: what work is it by which we embrace and hold onto Christ's death and resurrection? It cannot be any outward work at all, but only the everlasting faith within our hearts, the faith which alone – yes, entirely alone, and without any works - embraces Christ's death and resurrection when it is preached through the Gospel. Why all this ranting and raving, this crying heresy and burning at the stake, when the crux of the matter is clear and proves that faith alone, without works, is what embraces Christ's death and resurrection, and that the same death and resurrection are our life and our justification? Therefore, since it is so self-evidently the case that faith alone brings us life and justification, embraces them both and gives them to us, why not say so? It isn't heresy that faith alone embraces Christ and grants life, but apparently it is heresy to come out and say so.

---

[49] Luther uses 'become righteous' in the same sense as 'be justified'; see Background, Section 3.

Sind sie nit toll / tö̊richt vñ vnsinig? die sachẽ bekeñen sie fur recht / vñ straffen doch die rede võ der selbigen sache fur vnrecht / keinerley zu gleich / mus beide recht vñ vnrecht sein.

Auch bin ichs nicht allein / noch der erste / der da sagt / Allein der glaube mach gerecht / Es hat fur mir Ambrosius / Aug. vñ vil andere gesagt / Vñ wer S. Paulũ lesen vñ verstehen sol / der mus wol so sagen / vñ kan nit anders. Seine wort sind zu starck / vñ leidẽ kein / ja gar kein werck. Ists kein werck / so mus der glaube allein sein. O wie solt es so gar ein feine / besserliche / vnergerliche lere sein / weñ die leute lerntẽ / dz sie neben dem glauben / auch durch werck frum möchtẽ werden / Dz wer so vil gesagt / dz nicht allein Christus tod vnser sunde weg neme / sondern vnsere werck thettẽ auch etwz da zu / dz hies Christus tod fein geehret / das vnser werck ym hulffen / vñ köndtẽ das auch thun das er thut / auff das wir yhm gleich gut vñ starck weren. Es ist der Teuffel / der das blut Christi nicht kan vngeschendet lassen.

Weil nu die sache ym grũd selbs fodert / dz man sage / Allein d' glaub macht gerecht / Vñ vnser deutschẽ sprachẽ art / die solchs auch lernt also aus zusprechen. Habe dazu der Heiligẽ våter exẽpel / vñ zwinget auch die fahr d' leute / dz sie nit an den werckẽ hangẽ bleibẽ / vñ des glaubẽs feilẽ / vñ Christũ verlierẽ / sonderlich zu diser zeit / da sie so lang her der werck gewonet / vñ mit macht davon zu reissen sind. So ists nit allein recht / sondern auch hoch võ nötẽ / dz man auffs aller deutlichst vñ voligst eraus sage / Allein der glaube on werck macht frum / vnd rewet mich / das ich nit auch dazu gesetzt habe alle vñ aller / also on alle werck aller gesetz das es vol vnd rund eraus gesprochen were / darũb sols in meinẽ Newen Testament bleiben / vnd solten alle Papstesel toll vnd töricht werden / so sollen sie mirs nicht eraus bringen. Das sey yetzt dauon gnug /

How mad, crazy, and deranged these people are! They acknowledge the thing as right but condemn talking about the thing as wrong – nothing can be right and wrong at the same time!

And I'm not the only one, nor the first, to say that faith alone justifies: before me Ambrose, Augustine, and many others have said so too. And anyone who reads and understands St Paul is compelled to say the same, and cannot do otherwise. St Paul's words are too forceful to allow works, even a single one. If it isn't works it must be faith alone. Oh, what fine, edifying, unalarming teaching it would be if people learnt that they could become righteous through works as well as through faith! That would amount to saying that it is not only Christ's death that takes away our sin, but that our works also have something to do with it. What a fine way of honouring Christ's death it would be to say that our works could help him and could do what he did, making us his equal in strength and goodness! That is the talk of the devil, who cannot help profaning the blood of Christ.

So the core of the argument demands that we say, 'Faith alone justifies' and the way German works also tells us that this is the way to express it. At the same time I have the precedent of the Holy Fathers, and the risk to people also means that they should stop clinging to works, straying from faith, and losing Christ, particularly now that they have become so long accustomed to works and will have to be torn away from them by force. It is therefore not only right but also highly necessary to put it in the clearest and most comprehensive terms that faith alone without works makes us righteous, and I regret that I didn't add 'any' twice and say, 'without any works of any law' to bring it out as a full and complete expression. So it's going to stay in my New Testament, and even if every donkey in popedom goes berserk, I'm not letting them take it away. That'll do for now:

Weiter wil ich (so Gott gnade gibt) dauon reden ym buchlin de iustificatione.

Auff die andern frage / ob die verstorben Heiligen fur vns bitten. Darauff wil ich yetzt kuͤrtzlich antwortenn / denn ich gedenck einen sermon von den lieben Engeln auszulassen / darinn ich diß stuͤck weitter (wils Gott) handeln werde. Erstlich wisset yhr / das ym Bapstum nicht allein das geleret ist / das die Heiligen ym hymel fur vns bitten / Welchs mir doch nicht wissenn koͤnnen / weil die schrifft vns solchs nicht sagt / Sondern auch dz man die Heiligen zu Goͤtter gemacht hat / das sie vnser Patron haben muͤssen sein / die wir anruͤffen sollenn / Etlich auch die nye gewest sind / Vnd einem iglichen heiligen sonderliche krafft vnd macht zu geeigent / einem vber fewr / diesen vber wasser / diesenn vber pestilentz / fieber / vnd allerley plage / das Gott selbs hat gar muͤssig sein muͤssen / vnd die Heiligen lassen an seiner stat wirckē vnd schaffen. Disen grewel fuͤlen die Papisten yetzt wol / vnd ziehen heimlich die pfeiffen ein / putzen vnnd schmuͤcken sich nu mit dem furbitt der Heiligen. Aber diß wil ich ytzt auffschiebē. Aber was gillts / ob ichs vergessen / vnd solchs putzen vnd schmuͤcken also vngebuͤsset hin gehen lassen werde.

Zum andern / wisset yhr / das Gott mit keinem wort gebotten hat / wedder Engel noch Heiligen vmb furbit anzuruͤffenn / Habt auch yn der schrifft des kein exempel / denn man findet / das die lieben Engel mit den vaͤtern vnd propheten geredt haben / Aber nye keiner ist vor yhnen vmb furbit gebeten wordenn / Das auch der ertzuater Jacob seinenn kampffengel nicht vmb furbit bat / sondern nam allein den segen von yhm.[50] Man findet aber wol das widerspiel yn Apocalypsi / dz der Engel sich nicht wolt lassen anbetten von Joanne[51] / Vnnd findet sich also / das Heiligen dienst sey ein lauter menschen tandt / vnd ein eygen fuͤndlin ausser Gottes wort vnd der schrifft.

---

[50] Genesis 32: 24-9.

[51] Revelation 22: 8-9.

I'll have more to say on this, by the grace of God, in my treatise 'De iustificatione'.[52]

As for the other question, whether the departed saints pray for us, I'll give only a brief answer for the time being, because I'm planning to publish a sermon on our dear angels in which, God willing, I'll deal with the matter more fully. First, you know that under the papacy not only is it taught that the saints in heaven pray for us - which we actually have no way of knowing because Scripture tells us nothing of the sort -, but also the saints have been turned into Gods and forced to be our patrons, who we're meant to call upon, including some who have never existed. To each saint a particular power and authority is ascribed, one over fire, one over water, one over pestilence, disease, and all manner of plagues – indeed God himself must have been completely idle, letting the saints toil and sweat in his place. These days the papists are well aware what an abomination this is, so they pipe down about it, and now they primp and preen themselves on the doctrine of the intercession of saints. I'll put off this subject for now, but you can bet I won't forget it and I'm not going to allow their primping and preening to go unpunished.

Second, as you know, not a single word of God commands us to call upon either angels or saints to intercede for us. Nor is there any example of this in Scripture: we do find our dear angels conversing with the fathers and prophets, but no angel was ever asked by them to intercede. Even the patriarch Jacob didn't ask the angel he wrestled with for intercession, but just took the angel's blessing. In fact we find quite the opposite in Revelation, where the angel would not allow himself to be worshipped by John. So it turns out that the worshipping of saints is nothing but human nonsense, contrived by mankind without regard to the word of God and Scripture.

[52] 'On Justification'. This work was never completed, although preliminary material survives.

Weil vns aber yn Gotes dienst nichts gebuͤrt furzunemē on gottes befelh / Vn̄ wer es furnimpt / dz ist ein gottes versuchūg / Darumb ists nicht zu rathen noch zu leiden / das man die verstorbenn Heiligenn vmb furbitt anruͤffe / oder anruͤffen lere / sonder sols vil mehr verdamnen vn̄ meidē lerē / Derhalbē ich auch nicht dazu rathen / vn̄ mein gewissen mit frembder missethat nicht beschweren wil. Es ist mir selber aus der massen saür worden / dz ich mich von den Heiligen gerissen habe / den̄ ich vber alle masse tieff drinnen gesteckt vnd ersoffen gewest bin. Aber das liecht des Euangelij ist nu so helle am tag / das hinfurt niemand entschuldigt ist / wo er ym finsternis bleibt. Wir wissen fast alle wol / wz wir thun sollen.

Vber dz so ists an ym selbs ein ferlicher ergerlicher dienst / dz die leute gewonē gar leicht sich von Christo zu wenden / vn̄ lernē bald mehr zuuersicht auff die Heiligen / den̄ auff Christo selbs zu setzen / Den̄ es ist die natur on dz all zu seer geneigt von got vnd Christo zu fliehen / vn̄ auff menschen zu trawen / Ja es wird aus der massen schweer / das man lerne auff Got vn̄ Christū trawē / wie wir doch gelobt haben vnnd schuldig sind / Darumb ist solch ergernis nicht zu dulden / damit die schwachen vn̄ fleischlichen leute ein abgoͤterey anrichten / widder das erste gebot / vn̄ wider vnser tauffe. Man treibe nur getrost die zuuersicht vn̄ vertrawē vō den Heiligen zu Christo / beide mit leren vn̄ vben / es hat dennoch muͤhe vn̄ hindernis gnug / dz man zu jm kompt vn̄ recht ergreifft. Man darff den Teuffel nicht vber die thuͤr malē / Er findet sich wol selbs.

Zu letzt / sind wir ja gewiß / das got nicht drumb zurnet / vn̄ sind wol sicher / ob wir die Heiligen nicht vmb furbit anruͤffen / weil ers nirgent geboten hat / den̄ er spricht / dz er sey ein eyfferer / der die missethat heimsucht an denen / die sein gebot nicht halten[53] / Hie aber ist kein gebot / darūb auch keinn zorn zu furchten.

---

[53] Exodus 20: 5.

Since in matters of divine worship it is not right to do anything which is not commanded by God - and anyone doing so is tempting God - , it is neither advisable nor tolerable to call on the departed saints for intercession or to teach others to do so. Instead the practice should be condemned and people taught to avoid it, which is why I won't recommend it either, nor burden my conscience with the wrongs of others. It was extremely painful for me to tear myself away from the saints: I was so completely steeped in the practice, I was at drowning point. But now the light of the Gospel shines so brightly that no-one has an excuse for remaining in darkness any longer. We all know very well what we have to do.

Besides, it's a dangerous and alarming form of worship in itself if it means that people get accustomed very easily to turning away from Christ and soon learn to place more trust in the saints than in Christ himself. As it is, we are by nature only too ready to flee from God and Christ and place our trust in human beings. In fact it becomes exceedingly difficult to learn to trust in God and Christ, even though this is what we have promised and what we are obliged to do. So an abomination like this cannot be tolerated, one which leads those who are weak and of the flesh to start practising idolatry against the first commandment and against our baptism. Even if you simply urge people to switch their faith and trust from the saints to Christ through both teaching and example, it will still be a struggle and a challenge for them to come to him and grasp him properly. You don't need to paint the devil on the door - he'll find his own way in.

Finally, we can in fact be certain that God won't be angry about this and we will be quite safe if we don't call upon the saints for intercession, because God has never commanded it. He says that he is a jealous God, who visits their wrongs on those who don't keep his commandments, but there is no commandment here and so no wrath to be feared.

Weil deñ hie auff diser seiten sicherheit ist / vñ dort grosse fahr vñ ergernis wider gottes wort / Warũb wolten wir vns deñ aus der sicherheit begeben yn die fahr / da wir kein Gottes wort haben / das vns in der not / halten / trŏsten oder erretten kan? Deñ es stehet geschriben, Wer sich gern in die fahr gibt / der wird drinnen vmkomen.[54] Auch spricht gottes gebott / Du solt got deinen herrn nicht versuchen.[55]

Ja sprechen sie / damit verdampstu die gantzen Christenheit die allenthalben solchs bißher gehalten hat. Antwort / Ich weiß fast wol / dz die Pfaffen vñ Münich / solchen deckel yhrer grewel suchen / vñ wŏllen auff die Christenheit schieben / was sie verwarloset haben / Auff das / weñ wir sagẽ / die Christenheit yrre nicht / so sollen wir auch sagen / dz sie auch nicht yrren / vñ also kein lůgẽ auch yrrthum an yn můge gestrafft werden / weil es die Christẽheit so helt. Also ist deñ keine walfart (wie offenberlich der teufel da sey) kein ablas (wie grob die lůgen sey) vnrecht. Kurtzumb eytel heiligkeit ist da / Darumb solt yr hie zu so sagẽ / Wir handeln ytzt nicht wer verdampt odder nicht verdampt sei. Dise frembde sache mengen sie da her / dz sie vns von vnser sache furen / Wir hãdeln ytzt võ gottes wort / was die Christenheit sey oder thu / dz gehŏret auff ein ander ort. Hie fragt man / was gottes wort sey odder nit. Wz gottes wort nit ist / dz macht auch keine Christẽheit.

Wir lesen zur zeit Helie des propheten / dz offentlich kein gottes wort noch gottes dienst war ym gantzen volck Israel / wie er spricht / Herr sie habẽ deine prophetẽ getŏdt / vñ deine altar vmbgegraben / Vnd bin ich gar alleine.[56]

---

[54] Ecclesiasticus 3: 26 (Apocrypha).

[55] Deuteronomy 6: 16.

[56] 1 Kings 19: 10, 14.

Since, therefore, we have certainty on one side and great danger of offending against God's word on the other, why would we give up certainty and choose danger where we do not have the word of God to sustain us, comfort us, or save us in times of need? As it is written, 'Anyone who courts danger will die by it', and God's commandment says, 'You must not tempt the Lord your God'.

They will claim that in this way you condemn all Christians everywhere who have been observing this practice. My answer: I am well aware that priests and monks try to use this as cover for their abominations and to shift the blame onto all Christians for the damage caused by their own negligence – so that if we say Christians don't err we must therefore be saying that *they* don't err either, and therefore they cannot be punished for any lie or error since this is what Christians practise. This means that no pilgrimage (however obviously the devil is involved) and no indulgence[57] (however blatant the lies) can be wrong. In a word, it is all pure holiness. So your response should be that we're not dealing here with who is or isn't condemned. They smuggle in this irrelevant point to distract us from the matter at hand. We're dealing here with the word of God. What Christians are or do belongs elsewhere. Here the question is, 'What is or is not the word of God?' What is not the word of God has no part whatsoever in Christianity.

We read that in the days of the prophet Elijah there was no public preaching of God's word and no worship of God throughout the people of Israel. As Elijah says, 'Lord, they have slain your prophets and demolished your altars, and I am completely alone.'

---

[57] On the sale of indulgences, see Background, Section 3.

Hie wird der kȏnig Ahab vñ andere auch gesagt haben / Elia / mit solcher rede verdampstu dz gantz volck gottes. Aber gott hatte gleich wol sieben tausent behaltē.[58] Wie? Meinstu nit dz got vnter dem Bapstū ytzt auch habe kȏnnen die seinen erhalten / ob gleich die pfaffen vñ münche in der Christenheit eytel teufels lerer gewest / vnd in die hell gefaren sind? Es sind gar vil kinder vñ junges volck gestorbē in Christo / Deñ Christus hat mit gewalt vnter seinē Widerchrist die taufe dazu dē blossen text des Euangelij auff der cantzel / vñ dz Vater vnser / vñ den glauben erhalten / damit er gar viel seiner Christen vñ also seine Christenheit erhalten / vñ den teuffels lerern nichts dauon gesagt.

Vnd ob die Christen gleich haben etlich stůcke der Bȃpstlichen grewel gethan / so haben die Bapstesel damit noch nicht beweiset / das die lieben Christē solchs gern gethan haben / vil weniger ist damit beweiset / dz die Christen recht gethan haben. Christen kȏnnen wol yrren / vnd sundigen allesampt / Gott aber hat sie allesampt leren betten vmb vergebung der sunden ym vater vnser / vnd hat yhr solch sunde / die sie haben mussen / vngern / vnwissend / vñ von dem Widerchrist gezwungen thun / wol wissen zu vergeben / vnd dennoch pfaffen vñ mȗnchē nichts dauon sagē. Aber dz kan man wol beweisen / das yn aller welt ymer ein gros heimlich mummeln vnd klagen gewest ist widder die geistlichen / als giengen sie mit der Christenheit nicht recht vmb / Vnnd die Bapstesel haben auch solchem mummeln mit fewr vnd schwerd trefflich widerstanden biß auff dise zeit daher. Solch mummeln beweiset wol / wie gern die Christen solch grewel gesehen / vnnd wie recht man daran gethan habe.

[58] 1 Kings 19: 18.

At this point King Ahab and others might have said, 'Elijah, with that sort of talk you condemn all the people of God.' But at the same time God had spared seven thousand. How? Do you not think that God could also today, under the papacy, have preserved his own, even though the priests and monks within Christendom have been teaching nothing but the word of the Devil and gone to hell? A great many infants and children have died in Christ,[59] for even under the Antichrist[60] Christ has, through his power, preserved baptism, as well as the simple text of the Gospel read out from the pulpit, the Lord's Prayer, and the Creed, and in doing so he has preserved large numbers of *his* Christians and therefore *his* Christendom, without mentioning any of it to those who teach the Devil's word.

And even if Christians have contributed in some part to this papal abomination, the donkeys of popedom have not thereby proved that good Christians did so willingly, still less that they were right to do so. All Christians can undoubtedly err and sin, but God has taught them all to beg forgiveness for their sins in the Lord's Prayer, and He could very well have forgiven those sins which – unwillingly, unwittingly, or compelled by the Antichrist – they couldn't help committing, and yet without mentioning any of this to priests or monks. But it's easy to prove that throughout the world there has always been a great deal of private muttering and complaining against the clergy that they were not doing right by Christians. And the donkeys of popedom have valiantly resisted such muttering with fire and the sword - right down to the present day. This muttering is clear evidence of how happy Christians have been about such abominations, and how right it was to be involved in them.

---

[59] These are people too young to profess their faith who are saved by baptism and by prayer.

[60] Luther often referred to the Pope as 'the Antichrist'.

Ja lieben Båpstesel / komet nu her / vnd saget / Es sey der Christenheit lere / wz yr erstunckē / erlogen / vnd als die bößwichter vñ verrether der lieben Christenheit mit gewalt auffgedrungen / vñ als die Ertzmörder vil Christen drüber ermördet habt / zeugen doch alle buchstaben yn allen Bapsts gesetzen / das nichts aus willen vñ rath der Christenheit ye mals sey gelert / sonder eytel districte / precipiēdo mandamus ist da / das ist yhr heiliger geist gewest. Solch tyrranney hat die Christenheit müssen leiden / damit yhr das sacrament geraubt / vnd on yhr schuld / so yn gefencknus gehalten ist. Vnd die Esel wolten solch vnleidlich tyranney yhrs freuels vns ytzt fur ein willige that vnd exempel der Christēheit verkauffen / vñ sich so fein putzen. Aber es will ytzt zu lang werdenn. Es sey das mal gnug auff die frage / Ein andermal mehr / Vñ haltet mir meine lange schrifft zu gut. Christus vnser Herr sey mit vns allen. Amen.

Ex Eremo octaua Septembris. 1530.

Martinus Luther
Ewr guter freundt.

Dem Erbarn vnd fursichtigen N. meinem
günstigen herrn vnd freunde.

So out with it, you donkeys of popedom! Say that this is Christian teaching, this stinking pack of lies which you villains and traitors have forced on good Christians and which you have killed great numbers of them for, you wicked murderers. Why, every letter of every papal law is testimony that none of their teaching has ever reflected the will or consent of ordinary Christians. There is nothing there but *destricte precipiendo mandamus.*[61] That has been their Holy Spirit! Christians have had to endure such tyranny, which has robbed them of the sacrament, and they have been held captive by it through no fault of their own. And still the donkeys would palm off on us this intolerable tyranny of their own wickedness as a willing act and an example of Christian practice, and get away scot-free themselves. But this is getting too long. Let it do as an answer to your question for now – more another time. Excuse this long letter. May Christ our Lord be with us all. Amen.

From the Wilderness[62]

8 September 1530

Your good friend Martin Luther

To the honourable and wise 'N', my generous patron and friend

---

[61] Latin: 'We firmly instruct and command'; this is a phrase used in papal bulls.

[62] This is how Luther signed the letters he wrote from Coburg castle in 1530; see Background, Section 2.

Glossary of Names

St **Ambrose.** 339-397. A Roman Christian who became Bishop of Milan. Like St Augustine, he was a 'Father of the Church', whose orthodoxy in matters of scriptural interpretation was not in doubt.

Aristotle. 384-322 B.C. Greek philosopher whose works on logic and ethics Luther taught but later rejected.

St **Augustine.** 354-430. North African Christian who became Bishop of Hippo. Luther had been a monk in the Order of St Augustine. See St **Ambrose.**

Bungler (of Dresden). See **Emser.**

Matthäus Aurogallus. c 1490-1543. Professor of Hebrew at Wittenberg. Colleague of Luther's and collaborator on the translation of the Old Testament. Aurogallus is a Latinized version of his birth name Goldhahn (literally 'golden cock').

Johann **Dobeneck.** 1479-1552. Secretary to **George** of Saxony and opponent of Luther. Helped prepare the case against the Reformers at the Diet of Augsburg (see Background, Section 2). Luther's nickname of 'Rotzlöffel' (literally 'Snot-spoon' but translated here as 'Snotty-Nose') refers to an upstart youth, but it is an elaborate pun. Dobeneck came from Wendelstein near Nuremberg; the name 'Wendelstein' literally means 'winding stone' and Dobeneck called himself Johann Cochläus based on the Latin 'cochlea' which means 'snail' or 'spiral'. Luther plays on the similarity between this and the Latin word 'cochlear', meaning 'spoon'.

Hieronymus **Emser.** 1477-1527. Also referred to as 'Bungler of Dresden'. Court Theologian to Duke George of Saxony and antagonist of Luther's. Wrote a long critique of Luther's New Testament and in 1527 produced a corrected version of Luther's New Testament (see Background, Sections 3 and 4).

Johann **Faber** of Leutkirch. 1478-1541. Real name Johann Heigerlin. Once a friend of Erasmus's and supporter of the Reformers, he turned hostile in the early 1520s. Became Bishop of Vienna in 1530. Helped prepare the case against the Reformers at the Diet of Augsburg (see Background, Section 2). Called himself Faber after his father, a blacksmith (Latin 'faber' means 'craftsman'), and Luther mocks him by translating this into German as 'Schmidt'.

Duke **George** of Saxony. 1471-1539. Cousin of the Elector of Saxony and opponent of Luther. Demanded that in his territory Luther's German translation of the New Testament should be collected and burned, and later wrote a preface to Emser's New Testament which was hostile to Luther (see Background, Sections 2 and 3).

St **Jerome**. c 347-420. Translator of the Bible into Latin. His version, known as the 'Vulgate', was to become the Catholic Church's official text of the Bible. Luther likened himself to Jerome in that both were criticized by their contemporaries for their Bible translations.

Wenceslas **Linck**. 1483-1547. Close friend of Luther's from student days. Became Dean of the Faculty of Theology at Wittenberg and Vicar General of the Augustinian Order. Resigned in 1523 to follow Luther. Linck was the recipient of the *Sendbrief*, and his account of how it came into his possession was a fiction agreed with Luther (see Background, Section 2).

Philipp **Melanchthon**. 1497-1560. Professor of Greek at Wittenberg, and a friend, close colleague, and collaborator of Luther's on the translation of the Bible. A leading reformer who played a major part in the Diet of Augsburg (see Background, Section 2). 'Melanchthon' is a Hellenized version of his birth name Schwartzerdt (literally 'black earth').

Dr **Schmidt**. See Johann Faber of Leutkirch.

Dr **Snotty-Nose**. See Johann Dobeneck.

Ein sendbrieff D. M. Lutthers.

Von Dolmetzschen vnd Fürbit der heiligenn.

M·D·XXX·

Wenczeslaus Linck allen Christglaubigenn

GOttes gnad vnd barmhertzigkeit. Der weise Salomon spricht Prou. 11. Wer korn inhelt/dem fluchen die leute. Aber segē kompt vber den/so es verkaufft. Welcher spruch eigentlich zu vorstehen ist von allem das zu gemeinem nutze odder tröste der Christenheit dienen kan. Darumb schilt auch der Herr jm Euangelio den vntrewen knecht einen faulen schalck/das er sein gelt in die erden vergraben vnd verborgen hatte. Solchen fluch des herren vnd der gantzen gemein zu vermeiden/hab jch diesen sendtbrieff/der mir durch einen guten freundt zu handen kommen/nit wissen zu verhalten/sonder offentlich in druck geben/Dann die weil der verdolmetzschunge halben/altes vnnd newes testaments/vil rede sich zůtragen/Nemlich die feinde der warheit furgeben/sam were der text an vilen orten geendert/odder auch verfelschet/da durch viel einfeltige Christen/auch vntern gelerten/ßo der Hebreischen vnnd Grekischen sprache nit kundig/entsatzunge odder schew gewinnen/Ist gůttlich zu verhoffen das auffs minste zum teil hie mit den gottlosen/jhr lestern vorhindert/vnnd den frommen jhr scrupel benommen sollen werden/Villeicht auch verursachet/das ettwas mehrers auff solche fragstuck odder materi/geschriben werde/Bitt derhalben einen ieden liebhaber der warheit/wölle jhm sollich werck jm besten lassen entpfolhen sein/vnd Gott treulich bitten vmb rechten vorstandt der Göttlichen schrifft zu besserung vnnd mehe rung gmeiner Christenheit. Amen. Zu Nürmberg am 15. Septembris. Anno 1530.

Dem Erbarn vnd fursichtigen

N. meinem gůnstigen Herrn vnd freunde.

Gnad vnd fride in Christo/Erber fursichtiger lieber Herr vñ freund/ ich hab ewer schrifft entpfangen mit den zwo questionen odder fragen/ darin yhr meines berichts begert. Erstlich warumb ich zun Römern am dritten capitel/ die wort S. Pauli Arbitramur hominem iustificari ex fide absq; operibus/ also verdeutsch habe. Wir halten/ das der mensch gerecht werde on des gesetzs werck/allein durch den glauben/ Vñ zeigt danebē an/wie die Papisten sich vber die massen vnnůtze machen/ weil ym text Pauli nicht stehet das wort Sola (Allein) vnd sey solcher zusatz von mir nicht zu leiden ynn Gottes wortten etc. Zum andern/ob auch die verstorben Heiligen fur vns bitten/weil wir lesen/das ja die Engel fur vns bitten etc. Auff die ersten frage (wo es euch gelustet) můgt yr ewern Papisten von meinet wegē antworten also.

Zum ersten/Wenn ich D. Luther mich hette můgen des versehen/das die Papisten alle auff einen hauffen so geschickt werē/ dz sie ein Capitel yn der schrifft kůndten recht vnd wol verteutschen/So wolt ich furwar mich der demut haben finden lassen/vñ sie vmb hilff vnd beystand gebeten das Newe Testament zuuerteutschen. Aber die weil ich gewůst/vnd noch vor augen sihe/das yhr keiner recht weiß/wie man dolmetschen/odder teutsch reden sol/hab ich sie vnd mich solcher můhe vberhaben/ Das merckt man aber wol/das sie aus meinem dolmetschen vnd teutsch/lernen teutsch reden vñ schreiben/ vñ stelen mir also meine sprache/ dauon sie zuuor wenig gewist/dancken mir aber nicht dafur/sondern brauchen sie viel lieber wider mich. Aber ich gan es jn wol/ den es thut mir doch sanfft/dz ich auch meine vndāckbare jůnger

 dazu

dazu meine feinde reden gelert habe.

Zum andern mügt yhr sagen/ das ich das Newe Testamēt verdeutscht habe/ auff mein bestes vermügen vnd auff mein gewissen/ habe damit niemand gezwungen / das ers lese / sondern frey gelasen/ vnd allein zu dienst gethan denen/ die es nicht besser machen können/ Ist niemandt verboten ein bessers zu machen. Wers nicht lesen wil/ der las es ligen/ ich bite vnd feyre niemādt drumb. Es ist mein testament vnd mein dolmetschung / vnd sol mein bleiben vnnd sein. Hab ich drinnen etwa gefeilet (das mir doch nicht bewust/ vnd freilich vngern einen bůchstaben mütwilliglich wolt vnrecht verdolmetschen) darüber wil ich die Papistē nicht zu richter leiden/ denn sie haben noch zur zeit zu lange ohren dazu/ vnd yhr ycka ycka ist zu schwach mein verdolmetschen zu vrteilen/ Ich weiß wol/ vnd sie wissens weniger/ denn des Mülners thier/ was fur kunst/ fleiß/ vernunfft/ verstandt zum gutten dolmetscher gehöret/ denn sie habens nicht versůcht.

Es heist/ Wer am wege bawet/ der hat viel meister. Also gehet mirs auch. Die jhenigen die noch nye haben recht reden können/ schweige deñ dolmetschen/ die sind allzumal meine meister/ vnd ich mus yhr aller junger sein. Vnd wenn ich sie hette sollen fragen/ wie man die ersten zwey wort Matthei. 1. Liber Generationis solte verdeutschen/ so hette yhr keiner gewist gack dazu zu sagen/ Vnd vrteilen mir nu das gantze werck/ die feinen gesellē. Also giēg es S. Hieronymo auch/ da er die Biblia dolmetscht/ da war alle welt sein meister/ Er allein war es/ der nichts kunte/ Vnd vrteileten dem guten man sein werck/ die jhenigē / so ym nicht gnug gewest weren/ das sie ym die schuch hetten sollē wischen/ Darumb gehöret grosse gedult dazu/ so yemād etwas offentlich guts thun will/ denn die wellt wil meister klüglin bleiben/ vnd mus ymer das Ros vnter dem schwantz zeumen / alles meistern/ vnnd selbs nichts können / das ist yhr art / dauon sie nicht lassen kan.

Ich wolt noch gern den Papisten ansehē/ der sich erfur thet/ vnd etwa eine epistel S. Pauli oder einen Propheten verdeutschet/ So et/So fern/das er des Luthers teutsch vñ dolmetzschen nicht da zu gebraucht/da solt man sehen ein fein/schön/loblich deutsch od der dolmetzschen/Deñ wir haben ja gesehē den Sudler zu Drē sen/der mein New Testament gemeistert hat(ich wil seinen namen yn meinen büchern nicht mehr nennen/So hat er auch nun seinen richter/vnd ist sonst wol bekandt) der bekennet/das mein deutsch susse vnd gut sey/vnd sahe wol/das ers nicht besser machen kundt/vñ wolt es doch zu schandē machen/fur zu/vnd nam fur sich mein New Testament/fast von wort zu wort/wie ichs gemacht hab/vnd thet meine vorhede/gloß vnd namen dauon/schreib seinen namen/vorhede vnd gloß dazu/verkaufft also mein New Testament vnter seinem namen/Wañ liebē kinder/wie geschach mir da so wehe/da sein landsfurst mit einer grewlichen vorrhede verdampt/vnd verbot des Luthers New Testament zu lesen/Doch daneben gebot des Sudelers New Testament zu lesen/welchs doch eben dasselbig ist/das der Luther gemacht hat.

Vnd das nicht yemand hie dencke/ich liege/So nym beide Testament fur dich/des Luthers vnd des Sudelers/halt sie gegen ein ander/so wirstu sehē/wer yn allen beidē der dolmetzscher sey/Denn was er yn wenig orten geflickt vnd geendert hat(wie wol mirs nicht alles gefellet)So kan ichs doch wol leiden/vnnd schadet mir sonderlich nichts/so viel es den text betrifft/darumb ich auch nie da wider hab wöllen schreiben/sondern hab der grossen weißheit müssen lachen/das man mein New Testament so grewlich gelestert/verdampt/verboten hat/weil es vnter meinē namen ist außgangen/Aber doch müssen lesen/weil es vnter eines andern namen ist außgangen. Wie wol/was das fur ein tugent sey/einem andern sein büch lestern vnd schenden/darnach das selbige stelen/vnd vnter eigenem namen dennoch auß lassen gehen/vnd also durch frembde verlesterte erbeyt eygen lob vnd namen süchen/das las ich seinen richter finden. Mir ist ynn des gnug/vnd bin fro/das meine erbeit(wie S. Paulus auch rhümet)muß auch durch meine feinde gefördert/vnd des Luthers bůch on Luthers namen/vnter seiner feinde namen gelesen werden/ Wie künd ich mich bas rechen?

Vnd das ich wider zur sachen kome/ Wañ ewr Papist sich vil vnnütze machen wil mit dem wort (Sola Allein) so sagt jm flugs also / Doctor Martinus Luther wils also haben / vnnd spricht/ Papist vnd Esel sey ein ding. Sic volo/sic iubeo/sit pro ratione voluntas. Denn wir wöllen nicht der Papisten schuler noch jünger / sonder yhre meister vnd richter sein / Wöllen auch ein mal stoltziern vñ pochen mit den Esels köpffen/ vñ wie Paulus wider seine tollen Heiligen sich rhůmet / so wil ich mich auch widder diese meine Esel rhůmen. Sie sind doctores? Ich auch. Sie sind gelert? Ich auch. Sie sind Prediger? Ich auch. Sie sind Theologi? Ich auch. Sie sind Disputatores? Ich auch. Sie sind Philosopi? Ich auch. Sie sind Dialectici? Ich auch. Sie sind Legenten? Ich auch. Sie schreiben bůcher? Ich auch.

Vnd wil weiter rhůmen/ Ich kan Psalmen vnd Prophetē außlegen/ Das künnen sie nicht. Ich kan dolmetzschen/ Dz können sie nicht. Ich kan die heiligen schrifft lesen / Das können sie nicht. Ich kan biten/ Das können sie nicht. Vnd das ich herunter kome/ Ich kan yhr eygen Dialectica vnd Philosophia bas/ denn sie selbs allesampt. Vnd weiß dazu fur war / das yhr keiner yhren Aristotelem verstehet. Vnnd ist einer vnter yn allen der ein proemium odder Capittel ym Aristotele recht verstehet / so wil ich mich lassen prellen. Ich rede ytzt nicht zuuil/ deñ ich bin durch yhre kunst alle erzogen vnd erfaren von jugent auff/ weiß fast wol wie tieff vnd weit sie ist. So wissen sie auch wol / das ichs alles weiß vnd kan/ was sie können/ Noch handeln die heillosen leute gegen mir/ als were ich ein gast jnn yhrer kunst/ der aller erst heut morgen komen were/ vñ noch nie weder gesehen noch gehört hette/ was sie leren odder können/ So gar herrlich prangen sie herein mit yhrer kunst/ vnd leren mich/ was ich vor zwentzig jaren an den schuhen zu rissen habe/ das ich auch mit jhener metzen auff all yhr plerren vnd schreien singen mus / Ich habs fur siben jaren gewist/ das hůffnegel eysen sind.

Das

Das sey auff ewr erste Frag geantwortet/vn̄ bitte euch/wöllet solchen Eseln ja nicht anders noch mehr antworten auff yhr vnnütze geplerre/vom wort Sola / Denn also viel/ Luther wils so haben/vn̄ spricht/Er sey ein Doctor vber alle Doctor jm gantzen Bapstum/da sols bey bleiben/ Ich will sie hinfurt schlecht verachten/vnd veracht haben/so lange sie solche leute(ich wolt sagen) Esel sind/Denn es sind solche vnuerschempte tropffen vnter yhn/die auch yhr eigen der Sophisten kunst nye gelernt haben/wie Doctor Schmidt/vnd doctor Rotzlöffel/vnd seine gleichen/vnd legen sich gleich wol widder mich/yn dieser sachen / die nicht allein vber die sophisterey/sondern auch(wie sanct Paulus sagt)vber aller welt weißheit vnd vernunfft ist. Zwar es durfft ein Esel nicht viel singen/man kennet yn sonst wol bey den ohrē.

Euch aber vnd den vnsern wil ich anzeigen/ warumb ich dz wort(sola)hab wöllen brauchen/Wiewol Roma.3.nicht sola/ sondern solum odder tantum von mir gebraucht ist. Also fein sehen die Esel meinen text an. Aber doch hab ichs sonst anders wo sola fide gebraucht vn̄ wil auch beide solum vnd sola haben. Ich hab mich des geflissen ym dolmetzschen / das ich rein vnd klar teutsch geben möchte. Vnd ist vns wol offt begegnet / das wir viertzehen tage/drey/vier wochen haben ein einiges wort gesůcht vnd gefragt/habens dennoch zu weilen nicht funden. Jm Hiob erbeiten wir also/M. Philips / Aurogallus vnd ich/ das wir yn vier tagen zu weilen kaum drey zeilen kundten fertigen. Lieber/ nu es verdeutscht vn̄ bereit ist/kans ein yeder lesen vnd meistern/ Laufft einer ytzt mit den augen durch drey vier bletter vnd stost nicht ein mal an/wird aber nicht gewar welche wacken vnd klötze da gelegen sind/da er ytzt vber hin gehet/ wie vber ein gehoffelt bret/da wir haben müssen schwitzen vn̄ vns engsten / ehe den wir solche wacken vnd klotze aus dem wege reümeten / auff das man kündte so fein daher gehen. Es ist gut pflugen / wenn der acker gereinigt ist. Aber den wald vnd die stöcke aus rotten/ vnd dē acker zu richten/da will niemandt an. Es ist bey der welt kein danck zu verdienen/ Kan doch Got selbs mit der sonnen/ ja mit himel vnd erden/noch mit seines eigen sons tod keinen danck ver dienen/sie sey vñ bleibt welt deß teuffels namen/weil sie ja nicht anders will.

Also habe ich hie Roma.3.fast wol gewist/ das ym Lateini schen vnd krigischen text das wort(solum)nicht stehet/vnd hettẽ mich solchs die papisten nicht dürffen leren. War ists. Dise vier buchstaben s o l a stehen nicht drinnen / welche buchstaben die Eselsköpff ansehen/wie die kue ein new thor/Sehen aber nicht das gleichwol die meinung des text ynn sich hat/ vnd wo mans wil klar vnd gewaltiglich verteutschen/so gehoret es hinein/ deñ ich habe deutsch/nicht lateinisch noch kriegisch reden wöllen / da ich teutsch zu reden ym dolmetzschen furgenomen hatte. Das ist aber die art vnser deutschen sprache/wenn sie ein rede begibt/von zweyen dingen/der man eins bekennet/vñ das ander verneinet/ so braucht man des worts solum(allein)neben dem wort (nicht oder kein)Als wenn man sagt/Der Baür bringt allein korn vñ kein geldt/Nein/ich hab warlich ytzt nicht geldt / sondern allein korn. Ich hab allein gessen vnd noch nicht getruncken. Hastu allein geschrieben vnd nicht vberlesen? Vnd der gleichen vnzeliche weise yn teglichen brauch.

Jn disen reden allẽ/obs gleich die lateinische oder kriechische sprach nicht thut/so thuts doch die deutsche/vnd ist yhr art / das sie das wort(allein)hinzu setzt/auff das das wort (nicht odder kein)deste volliger vnd deutlicher sey/Denn wie wol ich auch sage/Der Baür bringt korn vñ kein geld/ So laut doch das wort (kein geldt)nicht so vollig vnd deutlich/als wenn ich sage / Der Baür bringt allein korn vnd kein geldt/ vnd hilfft hie das wort (Allein)dem wort(kein)so viel/das es ein vollige Deutsche klare rede wird/den man mus nicht die buchstaben inn der lateinischẽ sprachen fragẽ/wie man sol Deutsch redẽ/wie diese esel thun/sondern/man mus die mutter jhm hause/die kinder auff der gassen/ den gemeinen mã auff dem marckt drumb fragen/vñ den selbigẽ auff das maul sehen/wie sie reden/vnd darnach dolmetzschen/so verstehen sie es den/vñ mercken/das man Deutsch mit jn redet.

Als

Als wenn Christus spricht/ Ex abundantia cordis os loquitur. Wenn ich den Eseln sol folgen/ die werden mir die buchstaben furlegen/ vnd also dolmetzschen/ Auß dem vberflus des hertzen redet der mund. Sage mir/ Ist das deutsch geredt? Welcher deutscher verstehet solchs? Was ist vberflus des hertzẽ fur ein ding? Das kan kein deutscher sagen/ Er wolt denn sagen/ es sey das einer allzu ein gros hertz habe/ oder zu vil hertzes habe/ wie wol das auch noch nicht recht ist/ deñ vberflus des hertzen ist kein deutsch/ so wenig/ als das deutsch ist/ Vberflus des hauses/ vberflus des kacheloffens/ vberflus der banck/ sondern also redet die mutter ym haus vnd der gemeine man/ Wes das hertz vol ist/ des gehet der mund vber/ dz heist gut deutsch geredt/ des ich mich geflissen/ vñ leider nicht allwege erreicht noch troffen habe/ Deñ die lateinischẽ buchstabẽ hindern aus der massen seer gut deutsch zu reden.

Also/ weñ der verrether Judas sagt/ Matthei. 26. Vt quid perditio hec? Vnd Marci. 14. Vt quid perditio ista vngenti facta est? Folge ich den Eseln vnd buchstabilisten/ so mus ichs also verdeutschen/ Warumb ist dise verlierung der salben geschehen? Was ist aber das fur deutsch? Welcher deutscher redet also/ verlierung der salben ist geschehen? Vnd wenn ers wol verstehet/ so denckt er/ die salbe sey verloren/ vnd musse sie etwa wider suchen/ Wiewol das auch noch tunckel vnd vngewiß lautet. Wenn nu das gut deutsch ist/ warumb tretten sie nicht erfur/ vñ machen vns ein solch fein hubsch new deutsch Testament/ vñ lassen des Luthers Testament ligen? Ich meine ja sie solten yhre kunst an den tag bringen/ Aber der deutsche man redet also/ Vt quid ꝛc. Was sol doch solcher vnrat? odder/ was sol doch solcher schade? Nein/ Es ist schade vmb die salbe/ das ist gut deutsch/ daraus man verstehet/ das Magdalene mit der verschutten salben sey vnrethlich vmbgangen vnd habe schadenn gethan/ das war Judas meinung/ denn er gedacht bessern rat damit zu schaffen.

Item da der Engel Mariam grůsset vnd spricht/ Gegrůsset seistu Maria vol gnadẽ/ der Herr mit dir? Wolan/ so ists bißhet / schlecht den lateinischen buchstaben nach verdeutschet / sage mir aber ob solchs auch gut deutsch sey? Wo redet der deutsch man also / du bist vol gnaden? Vnd welcher Deutscher verstehet / was gsagt sey / vol gnaden? Er mus dencken an ein vas vol bier / oder beutel vol geldes / darumb hab ichs vordeutscht. Du holdselige / da mit doch ein Deutscher / dester meher hin zu kan dencken / was der engel meinet mit seinem grus. Aber hie wöllen die Papisten toll werden vber mich / das ich den Engelischen grus verderbet habe. Wie wol ich dennoch da mit nicht das beste deutsch habe troffen. Vnd hette ich das beste deutsch hie sollen nemen / vnd den grus also verdeutschen / Gott grusse dich du liebe Maria (denn so vil wil der Engel sagen / vnd so wurde er geredt haben / wan er hette wollen sie deutsch grussen) ich halt sie solten sich wol selbs erhenckt haben fur grosser andacht / zu der lieben Maria / das ich den grus so zu nichte gemacht hette.

Aber was frage ich darnach? sie toben oder rasen / ich wil nicht wehren / das sie verdeutschen was sie wöllen / ich wil aber auch verdeutschē / nicht wie sie wöllen / sonder wie ich wil / wer es nicht haben wil / der las mirs stehen / vñ halt seine meisterschafft bey sich / denn ich wil ir weder sehen noch hören / sie dorffen fur mein dolmetzschen nicht antwort geben / noch rechenschafft thun / Das hörestu wol / ich wil sagen / du holdselige Maria / du liebe Maria . vnd las sie sagen / du volgnaden Maria. Wer Deutsch kan / der weis wol / welch ein hertzlich fein wort das ist / die liebe Maria / der lieb Gott / der liebe Keiser / der liebe fürst / der lieb man / das liebe kind. Vnd ich weis nicht / ob man das wort liebe / auch so hertzlich vnd gnugsam in Lateinischer oder andern sprachen reden müg / das also dringe vnd klinge ynns hertz / durch alle sinne wie es thut in vnser sprache.

Denn ich halt S. Lucas als ein meister in Hebreischer vnd Greckischer sprache / hab das Hebreisch wort / so der Engel gebraucht / wöllen mit dem Greckischen kecharitomeni / treffen vnd deutlich geben. Vnd denck mir der Engel Gabriel habe mit Maria geredt / wie er mit Daniel redet / vnd nennet jnn Hamudoth vñ Isch Hamudoth/ vir desideriorum/ das ist/ du lieber Daniel. Denn das ist Gabrielis weise zu reden/ wie wir jhm Daniel sehen. Wenn ich nu den buchstaben nach/ aus der esel kunst/ solt des Engels wort verdeutschen/ muste ich also sagen/ Daniel du man der begirungen oder/ Daniel du man der lůste/ O das were schon deutsch/ Ein deutscher horet wol/ das Man/ Lůste/ oder begyrunge/ deutsche wort sind/ wie wol es nicht eytel reine deutsche wort sind/ sondern lust vnd begyr/ weren wol besser. Aber wenn sie so zusamen gefasset werden/ du man der begyrungen/ so weiß kein deutscher was gesagt ist/ denckt/ das Daniel villeicht vol böser lust stecke/ Das hiesse denn fein gedolmetzscht. Darumb mus ich hie die buchstaben faren lassen/ vnnd forschen/ wie der Deutsche man solchs redet/ welchs der Ebreische mã isch Hamudoth redet/ So finde ich/ das der deutsche mã also spricht/ Du lieber Daniel/ du liebe Maria/ oder du holdselige mad/ du medliche junckfraw/ du zartes weib/ vnd der gleichen. Deñ wer dolmetzschen wil/ mus grosse vorrath von worten haben/ das er die wol könne haben/ wo eins an allen orten nicht lauten will.

Vnd was sol ich vil vnd lange sagen von dolmetzschenn? Solt ich aller meiner wort vrsachen vnnd gedancken anzeigen/ ich müste wol ein jar dran zu schreiben haben. Was dolmetschen fur kunst vnd erbeit sey/ das hab ich wol erfaren/ darumb wil ich keinen papstesel noch maulesel/ die nichts versucht habẽ/ hierinn zum richter oder thadeller leiden. Wer mein dolmetzschen nicht wil/ der las es anstehen/ Der Teuffel dancke yhm/ wers vngerne hat oder on meinen willen vnd wissen meistert. Sols gemeistert werden/ so wil ichs selber thun. Wo ichs selber nicht thu/ da lasse man mir mein dolmetzschen mit friden/ vnd mache ein iglicher was er wil fur sich selbs/ vnd habe ym ein gut jar.

Das kan ich mit gutem gewissen zeugen/ das ich meine höchste trew vnd vleiß drinnen erzeigt/ vnd nye kein falsche gedanckẽ gehabt habe/ denn ich habe keinen heller da fur genomen noch gesůcht/ noch damit gewonnen/ So hab ich meine ehre drinnẽ nicht gemeinet/das weis Gott mein Herr/ sondern habs zu dienst gethan den lieben Christen/vnnd zu ehren einem der droben sitzet/ der mir alle stunde so vil guts thut/das wenn ich tausent mal so vil vnd vleissig gedolmetzscht/dennoch nicht eine stunde verdienet hette zu leben/odder ein gesundt auge zu haben/ Es ist alles seiner gnaden vñ barmhertzigkeit/was ich bin vnd habe/ Ja es ist seines theurē bluts vnd saüren schweißes/darumb sols auch (ob Gott wil) alles yhm zu ehren dienen/mit freuden vnnd von hertzen. Lestern mich die Sudeler vnd Bapstesel/wol an/so lobenn mich die frumen Christen sampt yhrem hern Christo/ Vnd bin allzu reichlich belohnet/wo mich nůr ein einiger Christ fur einen trewē erbeiter erkennet. Ich frag nach Bapsteseln nichts/sie sind nicht werd/das sie meine erbeit sollen erkennen / vnd solt mir ym grund meins hertzen leid sein/das sie mich lobetenn. Ihr lestern ist mein höhester rhům vñ ehr/ Ich will doch ein Doctor/ja auch ein ausbůndiger Doctor sein/vnd sie sollen mir den namen nicht nemen/ biß an den Jůngsten tag/ das weiß ich furwar.

Doch hab ich widerumb nicht allzu frey die buchstaben lassen faren/Sondern mit grossen sorgen sampt meinen gehůlffen drauff gesehen/das wo etwa an einem ort gelegenn ist / hab ichs nach den buchstaben behalten/vñ bin nicht so frey dauon gangē/ als Johannes .6. da Christus spricht/Disen hat Got der vatter versiegelt/da were wol besser deutsch gewest/Disen hat Gott d' vater gezeichent/odd' disen meinet Gott der vater. Aber ich habe ehe wöllen der deutschen sprache abbrechen/ denn von dem wort weichen. Ah es ist dolmetzschen ja nicht eines iglichen kunst / wie die tollen Heiligē meinē/Es gehöret dazu ein recht/frum/trew/ vleissig/forchtsam/Christlich/geleret/erfarn/geůbet hertz / Darumb halt ich/das kein falscher Christ noch rottengeist trewlich dolmetzschen könne/wie das wol scheinet inn den prophetenn zu Wormbs verdeutschet/darinn doch warlich grosser vleis geschehen/vnd meinem deutschen fast nach gangen ist. Aber es sind Jůden da bey gewest/die Christo nicht grosse hulde erzeigt haben/ sonst were kunst vnd vleiß genug da.

Das

Das sey vom dolmetzschen vñ art der sprachen gesagt. Aber
nu hab ich nicht allein der sprachen art vertrawet vnd gefolget/
das ich Roma.3. solum (Allein) hab hinzu gesetzt/ Sonder der
text vnd die meinung S. Pauli foddern vnd erzwingens mit ge
wallt/ denn er handelt ja daselbs das hauptstück Christlicher le=
re/ nemlich das wir durch den glauben an Christũ/ on alle werck
des gesetzs gerecht werden/ Vnd schneit alle werck so rein abe/ dz
er auch spricht/ des gesetzes (das doch Gottes gesetz vñ wort ist)
werck nicht helffen zur gerechtigkeit/ Vnd setzt zum exempel A=
braham/ das der selbige sey so gar on werck gerecht worden/ das
auch das höhest werck/ das dazu mal new gepotẽ ward von got
fur vnd vber allen andern gesetzen vnd wercken/ nemlich die be=
schneidung/ yhm nicht geholffen hab zur gerechtigkeit/ sonder sey
on die beschneidung vnd on alle werck gerecht worden durch den
glaubẽ wie er spricht Cap. 4. Ist Abraham durch werck gerecht
wordenn/ so mag er sich rhümen/ aber nicht fur Gott. Wo man
aber alle werck so rein abschneit/ vñ da mus ja die meinung sein/
das allein der glaube gerecht mache/ vnd wer deutlich vnd durre
von solchem abschneiden der werck redet wil/ der mus sagen/ Al
lein der glaube/ vnd nicht die werck machen vns gerecht/ dz zwin
get die sache selbs neben der sprachen art.

Ja sprechen sie/ Es laut ergerlich/ vnd die leute lernẽ daraus
verstehen/ das sie keine gute werck thun dürffen. Lieber was sol
man sagen? Ists nicht viel ergerlicher/ das S. Pauls selbs nicht
sagt/ allein der glaube/ sondern schuttets wol gröber eraus/ vnd
stosset dem faß den boden aus vnd spricht/ On des gesetzs werck/
Vnd Gala. 1. nicht durch die werck des gesetzes/ vñ des vil mehr
an andern orten/ denn das wort (allein der glaube) möcht noch
eine gloß findẽ/ Aber das wort (on werck des gesetzs) ist so grob/
ergerlich/ schendtlich/ das man mit keiner glossenn helffen kan/
Wie viel mehr möchten hieraus die leute lernen kein gute werck
thun/ da sie hören mit so durren starcken worten von den werckẽ
selbs predigen (Kein werck/ on werck/ nicht durch werck) ist nu dz
nicht ergerlich/ das mã (on werck/ kein werck/ nicht durch werck)

predigt/was solts den̄ ergerlich sein/so man diß (allein der glaube) predigt?

Vnd dz noch ergerlich ist/S. Paulus verwürfft nicht schlechte gemeine werck/sonder des gesetzes selbs. Daraus möchte wol yemand sich noch mehr ergern vnd sagen/Das gesetz sey verdāpt vnd verflucht fur Gott/ vnd man solle eytel böses thun / wie die theten Roman. 3. Last vns böses thun/ auff das es gut werde/ wie auch ein rotten geyst zu vnser zeit anfieng. Solt man vmb solcher ergernis willen S. Paulus wort verlaugnen/oder nicht frisch vnd frey vom glauben reden? Lieber eben S. Paulus vñ wir wöllen solch ergernis haben/vñ leren vmb keiner ander vrsachen willen/so starck wider die werck/ vñ treiben allein auff den glauben/das die leute sollen sich ergern/stossen vnd fallen/damit sie mugen lernen vñ wissen/das sie durch yr gute werck nit frum werden/sondern allein durch Christus tod vñ aufferstehẽ/ Können sie nu durch gute werck des gesetzes nicht frum werden/wie vil weniger werden sie frum werden durch böse werck vñ on gesetz/Darumb folget es nicht/Gute werck helffen nicht/darumb helffen böse werck/gleich als nicht fein folgt/ Die sonne kan dem blinden nicht helffen das er sehe/darumb mus ym die nacht vnd finsternis helffen/das er sehe.

Mich wundert aber/das man sich yn diser offentlichen sachẽ so mag sperrẽ. Sage mir doch/ob Christus tod vñ auffersteẽ vnser werck sey/das wir thun/oder nicht? Es ist ja nit vnser werck/ noch einiges gesetzes werck. Nu macht vns ja allein Christus tod vñ aufferstehen frey von sunden vñ frum/wie Paulus sagt Ro. 4. Er ist gestorbẽ vmb vnser sunde willen/vñ aufferstandẽ vmb vnser gerechtigkeit willẽ. Weiter sage mir/ Welchs ist dz werck/ damit wir Christus tod vñ aufferstehẽ fassen vñ haltẽ? Es mus ja kein eusserlich werck/sondern allein der ewige glaube ym hertzen sein/der selbige allein/ja gar allein/vnd on alle werck fasset solchen tod vñ aufferstehen wo es gepredigt wird durchs Euangelion. Was ists den̄ nu/dz man so tobet vñ wütet/ketzert vñ brẽnet/so die sach ym grundt selbs klerlich da ligt vnd beweiset/das allein

allein der glaube Chriſtus tod vñ aufferſtehē faſſe on alle werck/ vnd der ſelbige tod vñ aufferſtehen ſey vnſer leben vnd gerechtigkeit. So es deñ an ym ſelbs offentlich alſo iſt/ dz allein der glaube vns ſolch lebē vñ gerechtigkeit bringet/ faſſet vñ gibt/ Warūb ſoll man deñ nicht auch alſo redē? Es iſt nit ketzerey/ dz der glaube allein Chriſtū faſſet/ vñ das leben gibt/ Aber ketzerey muß es ſein wer ſolchs ſagt od' redet. Sind ſie nit toll/ töricht vñ vnſinig? die ſachē bekeñen ſie fur recht/ vñ ſtraffen doch die rede võ der ſelbigen ſache fur vnrecht/ keinerley zu gleich/ mus beide recht vñ vnrecht ſein.

Auch bin ichs nicht allein/ noch der erſte/ der da ſagt/ Allein der glaube mach gerecht/ Es hat fur mir Ambroſius/ Aug. vñ vil andere geſagt/ Vñ wer S. Paulū leſen vñ verſtehen ſol/ der mus wol ſo ſagen/ vñ kan nit anders. Seine wort ſind zu ſtarck/ vñ leidē kein/ ja gar kein werck. Iſts kein werck/ ſo mus der glaube allein ſein. O wie ſolt es ſo gar ein feine/ beſſerliche/ vnergerliche lere ſein/ weñ die leute lerntē/ dz ſie neben dem glauben/ auch durch werck frum möchtē werden/ Dz wer ſo vil geſagt/ dz nicht allein Chriſtus tod vnſer ſunde weg neme/ ſondern vnſere werck thettē auch etwz da zu/ dz hies Chriſtus tod fein geehret/ das vnſer werck ym hulffen/ vñ köndtē das auch thun das er thut/ auff das wir yhm gleich gut vñ ſtarck weren. Es iſt der Teuffel/ der das blut Chriſti nicht kan vngeſchendet laſſen.

Weil nu die ſache ym grūd ſelbs fodert/ dz man ſage/ Allein d' glaub macht gerecht/ Vñ vnſer deutſchē ſprachē art/ die ſolchs auch lernt alſo aus zuſprechen. Habe dazu der Heiligē väter exēpel/ vñ zwinget auch die fahr d' leute/ dz ſie nit an den werckē hangē bleibē/ vñ des glaubēs feilē/ vñ Chriſtū verlierē/ ſonderlich zu diſer zeit/ da ſie ſo lang her der werck gewonet/ vñ mit macht davon zu reiſſen ſind. So iſts nit allein recht/ ſondern auch hoch võ nötē/ dz man auffs aller deutlichſt vñ voligſt eraus ſage/ Allein der glaube on werck macht frum/ vnd rewet mich/ das ich nit auch dazu geſetzt habe alle vñ aller/ alſo on alle werck aller geſetz das es vol vnd rund eraus geſprochen were/ darūb ſols in meinē

Newē

Newen Testament bleiben/vnd solten alle Papstesel toll vnd tö richt werden/so sollen sie mirs nicht eraus bringen. Das sey yetzt dauon gnug/Weiter wil ich(so Gott gnade gibt) dauon reden ym buchlin de iustificatione.

Auff die andern frage/ob die verstorben Heiligen fur vns bitten. Darauff wil ich yetzt kürtzlich antwortenn/denn ich gedenck einen sermon von den lieben Engeln auszulassen / darinn ich diß stück weitter(wils Gott)handeln werde. Erstlich wisset yhr/das ym Babstum nicht allein das geleret ist/das die Heiligen ym hymel fur vns bitten/ Welchs mir doch nicht wissenn können/weil die schrifft vns solchs nicht sagt/ Sondern auch dz man die Heiligen zu Götter gemacht hat/das sie vnser Patron haben müssen sein/die wir anrüffen sollenn/ Etlich auch die nye gewest sind/Vnd einem iglichen heiligen sonderliche krafft vnd macht zu geeigent/einem vber fewr/ diesen vber wasser/ diesenn vber pestilentz/fieber/vnd allerley plage/das Gott selbs hat gar müssig sein müssen/vnd die Heiligen lassen an seiner stat wircke̅ vnd schaffen. Disen grewel fülen die Papisten yetzt wol/ vnd ziehen heimlich die pfeiffen ein/putzen vnnd schmücken sich nu mit dem furbitt der Heiligen. Aber diß wil ich yzt auffschiebe̅. Aber was gillts/ob ichs vergessen/vnd solchs putzen vnd schmücken also vngebüsset hin gehen lassen werde.

Zum andern/wisset yhr/das Gott mit keinem wort gebotten hat/wedder Engel noch Heiligen vmb furbit anzurüffenn/ Habt auch yn der schrifft des kein exempel / denn man findet/ das die lieben Engel mit den vätern vnd propheten geredt haben/Aber nye keiner ist vor yhnen vmb furbit gebeten wordenn/ Das auch der ertzuater Jacob seinenn kampffengel nicht vmb furbit bat/sondern nam allein den segen von yhm. Man findet aber wol das widerspiel yn Apocalypsi/dz der Engel sich nicht wolt lassen anbetten von Joanne/Vnnd findet sich also / das Heiligen dienst sey ein lauter menschen tandt/vnd ein eygen fündlin ausser Gottes wort vnd der schrifft.

Weil

Weil vns aber yn Gotes dienst nichts gebůrt furzunemē on
gottes befelh/ Vñ wer es furnimpt/ dz ist ein gottes versuchũg/
Darumb ists nicht zu rathen noch zu leiden/das man die verstor
benn Heiligenn vmb furbitt anrůffe/oder anrůffen lere/ sonder
sols vil mehr verdamnen vñ meidē lerē/ Derhalbē ich auch nicht
dazu rathen/vñ mein gewissen mit frembder missethat nicht be
schweren wil. Es ist mir selber aus der massen saür worden/ dz
ich mich von den Heiligen gerissen habe/deñ ich vber alle masse
tieff drinnen gesteckt vnd ersoffen gewest bin. Aber das liecht des
Euangelij ist nu so helle am tag/das hinfurt niemand entschul
digt ist/wo er ym finsternis bleibt. Wir wissen fast alle wol/wz
wir thun sollen.

Vber dz so ists an ym selbs ein ferlicher ergerlicher dienst/ dz
die leute gewonē gar leicht sich von Christo zu wenden/ vñ lernē
bald mehr zuuersicht auff die Heiligen/deñ auff Christo selbs zu
setzen/Deñ es ist die natur on dz all zu seer geneigt von got vnd
Christo zu fliehen/vñ auff menschen zu trawen/ Ja es wird aus
der massen schweer/das man lerne auff Got vñ Christũ trawē/
wie wir doch gelobt haben vnnd schuldig sind/Darumb ist solch
ergernis nicht zu dulden/damit die schwachen vñ fleischlichen leu
te ein abgöterey anrichten/widder das erste gebot/vñ wider vn=
ser tauffe. Man treibe nur getrost die zuuersicht vñ vertrawē vō
den Heiligen zu Christo/beide mit leren vñ vben/es hat dennoch
můhe vñ hindernis gnug/dz man zu jm kompt vñ recht ergreifft
Man darff den Teuffel nicht vber die thůr malē/ Er findet sich
wol selbs.

Zu letzt/sind wir ja gewiß/das got nicht drumb zurnet/ vñ
sind wol sicher/ob wir die Heiligen nicht vmb furbit anrůffen/
weil ers nirgent geboten hat/deñ er spricht/ dz er sey ein eyfferer/
der die missethat heimsůcht an denen/die sein gebot nicht halten/
Hie aber ist kein gebot/darūb auch keinn zorn zu furchten. Weil
deñ hie auff diser seiten sicherheit ist/ vñ dort grosse fahr vñ erger
nis wider gottes wort/ Warūb wolten wir vns deñ aus der sich
erheit begeben yn die fahr/da wir kein Gottes wort haben/ das
vns in der not/halten/trösten oder erretten kan: Deñ es stehet ge

schriben/ Wer sich gern in die fahr gibt/der wird drinnen vmko men. Auch spricht gottes gebott/ Du solt got deinen herrn nicht versuchen.

Ja sprechen sie/damit verdampstu die gantzen Christenheit die allenthalben solchs bißher gehalten hat. Antwort/ Ich weiß fast wol/dz die Pfaffen vñ Münich/ solchen deckel yhrer grewel suchen/vñ wöllen auff die Christenheit schieben/ was sie verwar loset haben/ Auff das/weñ wir sagẽ/die Christenheit yrre nicht/ so sollen wir auch sagen/dz sie auch nicht yrren/ vñ also kein lügẽ auch yrrthum an yn müge gestrafft werden/ weil es die Christẽ heit so helt. Also ist deñ keine walfart(wie offenberlich der teufel da sey)kein ablas(wie grob die lügen sey)vnrecht. Kurtzumb eytel heiligkeit ist da/ Darumb solt yr hie zu solsagẽ/ Wir handeln ytzt nicht wer verdampt odder nicht verdampt sei. Dise frembde sache mengen sie da her/dz sie vns von vnser sache furen/ Wir hãdeln ytzt võ gottes wort/was die Christenheit sey oder thu/dz gehöret auff ein ander ort. Hie fragt man/was gottes wort sey odder nit. Wz gottes wort nit ist/dz macht auch keine Christẽheit.

Wir lesen zur zeit Helie des propheten/dz offentlich kein gottes wort noch gottes dienst war ym gantzen volck Israel/wie er spricht/ Herr sie habẽ deine prophetẽ getödt/vñ deine altar vmbgegraben/ Vnd bin ich gar alleine. Hie wird der könig Ahab vñ andere auch gesagt haben/ Elia/mit solcher rede verdampstu dz gantz volck gottes. Aber gott hatte gleich wol sieben tausent behaltẽ. Wie? Meinstu nit dz got vnter dem Bapstũ ytzt auch habe können die seinen erhalten/ob gleich die pfaffen vñ münche in der Christenheit eytel teufels lerer gewest/vnd in die hell gefaren sind? Es sind gar vil kinder vñ junges volck gestorbẽ in Christo/ Deñ Christus hat mit gewalt vnter seinẽ Widerchrist die taufe dazu dẽ blossen text des Euangelij auff der cantzel/vñ dz Vater vnser/vñ den glauben erhalten/damit er gar viel seiner Christen vñ also seine Christenheit erhalten/vñ den teuffels lerern nichts dauon gesagt.

Vnd ob die Christen gleich haben etlich stücke der Bäpstlichen grewel gethan/so haben die Bapstesel damit noch nicht beweiset

weiset/das die lieben Christe solchs gern gethan haben/vñ weniger ist damit beweiset/dz die Christen recht gethan haben. Christen können wol yrren/vnd sundigen allesampt/ Gott aber hat sie allesampt leren betten vmb vergebung der sunden ym vater vnser/vnd hat yhr solch sunde/die sie haben mussen/vngern/ vnwissend/vñ von dem Widerchrist gezwungen thun/wol wissen zu vergeben/vnd dennoch pfaffen vñ münchē nichts dauon sagē. Aber dz kan man wol beweisen/das yn aller welt ymer ein gros heimlich mummeln vnd klagen gewest ist widder die geistlichen als giengen sie mit der Christenheit nicht recht vmb/ Vnnd die Babstesel haben auch solchem mummeln mit fewr vnd schwerd trefflich widerstanden biß auff dise zeit daher. Solch mummeln beweiset wol/wie gern die Christen solch grewel gesehen/ vnnd wie recht man daran gethan habe. Ja lieben Bäpstesel/ komet nu her/vnd saget/Es sey der Christenheit lere/ wz yr erstunckē/ erlogen/vnd als die böß wichter vñ verrether der lieben Christenheit mit gewalt auffgedrungen/vñ als die Ertzmörder vil Christen drüber ermördet habt/zeugen doch alle buchstaben yn allen Bapsts gesetzen/das nichts aus willen vñ rath der Christenheit ye mals sey gelert/sonder eytel districte/ precipiēdo mandamus ist da/das ist yhr heiliger geist gewest. Solch tyrranney hat die Christenheit müssen leiden/damit yhr das sacrament geraubt/ vnd on yhr schuld/so yn gefencknus gehalten ist. Vnd die Esel wolten solch vnleidlich tyranney yhrs freuels vns ytzt fur ein willige that vnd exempel der Christēheit verkauffen/ vñ sich so fein putzen. Aber es will ytzt zu lang werdenn. Es sey das mal gnug auff die frage/ Ein andermal mehr/ Vñ haltet mir meine lange schrifft zu gut. Christus vnser Herr sey mit vns allen. Amen. Ex Eremo octaua Septembris. 1 5 3 0.

Martinus Luther
Ewr guter freundt.

Dem Erbarn vnd fursichtigen N. meinem gūnstigen herrn vnd freunde.

F20

www.ingramcontent.com/pod-product-compliance
Lightning Source LLC
Chambersburg PA
CBHW071011120726
47910CB00004B/1470

* 9 7 8 0 9 9 5 4 5 6 4 1 9 *